James Stuart Candlish

Christian doctrine of God

James Stuart Candlish

Christian doctrine of God

ISBN/EAN: 9783337263317

Printed in Europe, USA, Canada, Australia, Japan

Cover: Foto ©Lupo / pixelio.de

More available books at **www.hansebooks.com**

From the Library of

Professor Benjamin Breckinridge Warfield

Bequeathed by him to

the Library of

Princeton Theological Seminary

```
BR 45 .H36 v.13
Candlish, James Stuart, 1835
 -1897.
Christian doctrine of God
```

Handbooks for Bible Classes and Private Students.

EDITED BY
REV. PROFESSOR MARCUS DODS, D.D.,
AND
REV ALEXANDER WHYTE, D.D.

NOW READY.

THE EPISTLE TO THE GALATIANS. By JAMES MACGREGOR, D.D., late of New College, Edinburgh. *Price 1s. 6d.*

THE POST-EXILIAN PROPHETS. With Introductions and Notes. By Rev. Prof. MARCUS DODS, D.D. *Price 2s.*

A LIFE OF CHRIST. By Rev. JAMES STALKER, D.D. *Price 1s. 6d.*

THE SACRAMENTS. By Rev. Professor CANDLISH, D.D. *Price 1s. 6d.*

THE BOOKS OF CHRONICLES. By Rev. Professor MURPHY, LL.D., Belfast. *Price 1s. 6d.*

THE CONFESSION OF FAITH. By Rev. JOHN MACPHERSON, M.A., Findhorn. *Price 2s.*

THE BOOK OF JUDGES. By Rev. Principal DOUGLAS, D.D. *Price 1s. 3d.*

THE BOOK OF JOSHUA. By Rev. Principal DOUGLAS, D.D. *Price 1s. 6d.*

THE EPISTLE TO THE HEBREWS. By Rev. Professor DAVIDSON, D.D., Edinburgh. *Price 2s. 6d.*

SCOTTISH CHURCH HISTORY. By Rev. N. L. WALKER, D.D. *Price 1s. 6d.*

THE CHURCH. By Rev. Prof. BINNIE, D.D., Aberdeen. *Price 1s. 6d.*

THE REFORMATION. By Rev. Professor LINDSAY, D.D. *Price 2s.*

THE BOOK OF GENESIS. By Rev. Prof. MARCUS DODS, D.D. *Price 2s.*

THE EPISTLE TO THE ROMANS. By Rev. Principal BROWN, D.D., Aberdeen. *Price 2s.*

PRESBYTERIANISM. By Rev. JOHN MACPHERSON, M.A. *Price 1s. 6d.*

LESSONS ON THE LIFE OF CHRIST. By Rev. WM. SCRYMGEOUR, Glasgow. *Price 2s. 6d.*

THE SHORTER CATECHISM. By Rev. ALEXANDER WHYTE, D.D., Edinburgh. *Price 2s. 6d.*

THE GOSPEL ACCORDING TO ST. MARK. By Rev. Professor LINDSAY, D.D., Glasgow. *Price 2s. 6d.*

A SHORT HISTORY OF CHRISTIAN MISSIONS. By GEORGE SMITH, LL.D., F.R.G.S. *Price 2s. 6d.*

A LIFE OF ST. PAUL. By Rev. JAMES STALKER, D.D. *Price 1s. 6d.*

PALESTINE. With Maps. By Rev. ARCH. HENDERSON, D.D., Crieff. *Price 2s. 6d.*

[Continued on next page.

THE BOOK OF ACTS. By Rev. Professor LINDSAY, D.D. Two Parts. *Price 1s. 6d. each.*

THE WORK OF THE HOLY SPIRIT. By Rev. Professor CANDLISH, D.D. *Price 1s. 6d.*

THE SUM OF SAVING KNOWLEDGE. By Rev. JOHN MACPHERSON, M.A., Findhorn. *Price 1s. 6d.*

HISTORY OF THE IRISH PRESBYTERIAN CHURCH. By Rev. THOMAS HAMILTON, D.D., Belfast. *Price 2s.*

THE GOSPEL ACCORDING TO ST. LUKE. By Rev. Professor LINDSAY, M.A., D.D. Part I., *price 2s.* Part II., *price 1s. 3d.*

THE CHRISTIAN MIRACLES AND THE CONCLUSIONS OF SCIENCE. By Rev. W. D. THOMSON, M.A., Lochend. *Price 2s.*

BUTLER'S THREE SERMONS ON HUMAN NATURE. With Introduction and Notes. By Rev. T. B. KILPATRICK, B.D. *Price 1s. 6d.*

THE CHRISTIAN DOCTRINE OF GOD. By Professor CANDLISH, D.D. *Price 1s. 6d.*

THE BOOK OF EXODUS. By JAMES MACGREGOR, D.D., late of New College, Edinburgh. Two Parts. *Price 2s. each.*

THE GOSPEL ACCORDING TO ST. JOHN. By Rev. GEORGE REITH, M.A., Glasgow. Two Parts. *Price 2s. each.*

CHURCH AND STATE. A Historical Handbook. By A. TAYLOR INNES, Esq., Advocate, Edinburgh. *Price 3s.*

THE MINOR PROPHETS. By Rev. Principal DOUGLAS, D.D. *Price 1s. 6d.*

THE BIBLICAL DOCTRINE OF SIN. By Rev. Professor CANDLISH, D.D.

IN PREPARATION.

THE SABBATH. By Rev. Professor SALMOND, D.D., Aberdeen.

THE FIRST EPISTLE TO THE CORINTHIANS. By Rev. Prof. MARCUS DODS, D.D.

THE SECOND EPISTLE TO THE CORINTHIANS. By Rev. Principal DAVID BROWN, D.D., Aberdeen.

THE EPISTLE TO THE PHILIPPIANS. By Rev. JAMES MELLIS, M.A., Southport.

THE EPISTLE TO THE COLOSSIANS. By Rev. SIMEON R. MACPHAIL, M.A., Liverpool.

CHRISTIAN ETHICS. By Rev. Professor LINDSAY, D.D., Glasgow.

APOLOGETICS. By Rev. Professor IVERACH, M.A., Aberdeen.

I. and II. PETER, and JUDE. By Rev. WM. PATRICK, B.D., Kirkintilloch.

THE PERSON OF CHRIST. By Rev. JAMES MACGREGOR, D.D.

CHURCH HISTORY. By Rev. Professor LINDSAY, D.D.

HANDBOOKS

FOR

BIBLE CLASSES

AND PRIVATE STUDENTS.

EDITED BY

PROFESSOR MARCUS DODS, D.D.,

AND

REV. ALEXANDER WHYTE, D.D.

THE BIBLICAL DOCTRINE OF SIN.
BY PROFESSOR J. S. CANDLISH, D.D.

EDINBURGH:
T. CLARK, 38 GEORGE STREET.
1893.

PRINTED BY MORRISON AND GIBB,

FOR

T. & T. CLARK, EDINBURGH.

LONDON : SIMPKIN, MARSHALL, HAMILTON, KENT, AND CO. LIMITED.

NEW YORK: CHARLES SCRIBNER'S SONS.

TORONTO: THE PRESBYTERIAN NEWS CO.

THE BIBLICAL DOCTRINE OF SIN.

BY

JAMES S. CANDLISH, D.D.,

PROFESSOR OF SYSTEMATIC THEOLOGY IN THE FREE CHURCH COLLEGE, GLASGOW.

EDINBURGH:
T. & T. CLARK, 38 GEORGE STREET.
1893.

CONTENTS.

CHAP.		PAGE
I.	THE BIBLICAL CONCEPTION OF SIN,	9
II.	COMPARISON OF VIEWS OF OTHER RELIGIONS,	18
III.	EVIDENCE OF THE TRUTH OF THE BIBLICAL VIEW,	31
IV.	THE NOTION OF GUILT CONNECTED WITH SIN,	38
V.	THE PUNISHMENT OF SIN,	45
VI.	THE UNIVERSALITY OF SIN IN MANKIND,	55
VII.	VARIOUS EXPLANATIONS OF THE UNIVERSALITY OF SIN,	69
VIII.	THE BIBLICAL DOCTRINE OF THE FALL OF MAN,	82
IX.	THE BIBLICAL DOCTRINE OF NATIVE DEPRAVITY,	90
X.	INABILITY OF MAN TO DELIVER HIMSELF,	99
XI.	THE INHERITANCE AND IMPUTATION OF SIN,	111
XII.	ELEMENTS OF HOPE IN MAN'S SINFUL STATE,	123

THE BIBLICAL DOCTRINE OF SIN.

CHAPTER I.

THE BIBLICAL CONCEPTION OF SIN.

CHRISTIANITY is in its essential nature remedial; it is not a mere benefit bestowed to increase the wellbeing of men; it is a deliverance, and indeed the only deliverance, from a most terrible and deadly evil; and that evil is, throughout the pages of Revelation, described as having its root and chief part in sin. The founder of Christianity was called Jesus, because He should save His people from their sin; He was hailed as "the Lamb of God, that taketh away the sin of the world"; He declared that He came to call sinners to the kingdom of God; and it is proclaimed as a faithful saying among His disciples "that Jesus Christ came into the world to save sinners." Entirely consistent with this are the anticipations and promises of the Old Testament. In the Law, the Prophets, and the Psalms, sin is recognised as the radical and greatest evil from which man needs to be saved.

Yet the Bible gives no didactic explanation of what sin is, but from the very outset of its teaching assumes that to be known. Just as the inspired writers do not think it needful to begin with a definition of God or a proof of His existence, as little do they count this necessary in regard to sin. For the practical purpose, which is the immediate object of revelation, neither was required; and the Word of God has met with a response in the consciences and hearts of men, when it addresses them as sinners, and calls them to return to God. Sin is a reality, and is felt as such, even though its nature be not explained to the intellect.

But in a systematic study of Bible teaching we need to have a clear and definite view of what sin is; and for that purpose we must inquire, How do we get that knowledge of it which the Bible assumes that we have? In seeking an answer to this question, we may begin with its most general conception, and advance from that to its specific character.

In its most general conception, sin is unquestionably an evil, and we get the notion of evil in general from our feeling. As capable of enjoyment and suffering, of happiness and misery, of desire and aversion, we have the notion of evil, including all that we dislike and fear, all that affects disagreeably our bodily, mental, or spiritual feelings; and as our experience enlarges, we include in the notion of evil all that leads, or may lead, to such disagreeable feelings. This general conception we have, simply as sentient beings.

But more specifically, as possessing conscience, or moral judgment, we have the notion of moral evil; and sin undoubtedly comes under this more specific conception. We know and judge our own actions, desires, and emotions, as right or wrong; we have an apprehension of what we ought to do and to be, and whatever deviates from that we pronounce to be morally evil and blameworthy. This constitutes a distinct kind of evil, different from other things that come under the general notion. Its difference, or special characteristic, lies in its being what ought not to be, what is wrong, what deserves blame and condemnation. What is the ground and origin of this moral judgment is a question disputed by philosophers; but it suffices us in the meantime to know that it is a real fact, and that it serves to define more precisely the notion of sin.

Man has, however, also a religious faculty, by which he comes into conscious relation to God; and this gives to moral evil the distinctive character of sin, under which it is always viewed in the Bible. <u>Sin is moral evil viewed as an offence against God.</u>

That the Bible uniformly recognises the notion of moral evil as sin against God hardly needs to be proved by citation of particular passages; but for the sake of distinctness reference may be made to some outstanding points in the evidence by which this is made plain. In the narratives of the times before Moses, the wickedness of man is represented as grieving God, and calling down His judgment (Gen. vi. 5–7); blood murderously shed cries to God (*ib.* iv. 10); the fear of God is thought by Abraham to be the only restraint upon injustice (*ib.* xxii. 11); and Joseph resists temptation to vice by the thought that it is a sin against God (*ib.* xxxix. 9). In the earliest part of the laws of Israel, the Book of the Covenant (Ex. xxi.–xxiii.), oppression and wrong are denounced as offences against God (*ib.* xxii. 23, 24), and the whole code is sanctioned by His authority. In the Levitical legislation, the prescriptions about sin and guilt offerings (Lev. iv., v.) imply the same idea; and especially in the laws of holiness, vice and crime are described as provoking God's wrath (Lev. xviii., xix.). The great work of the prophets was to proclaim that moral evil estranged men from God, and provoked His anger, in spite of the most costly and careful outward service (see *e.g.* Amos v., Hos. vi., Micah vi., Isa. i. etc.); and we have the response to that teaching in the utterances of penitent devotion in Ps. xxxii., l., li., cxxx., cxliii. With all this teaching before Christ's advent, the notion of moral evil as an offence against God was indelibly impressed on the Jewish mind; and our Lord and His apostles did not need to enforce it, but assumed it as an admitted and certain truth, and based on it the proclamation of forgiveness, peace with God, the enjoyment of His favour, and the hope of His glory, as a message of glad tidings to men who had all sinned and come short of the glory of God.

We generally define this aspect of moral evil by distinguishing it from others; and as when we view it as injuring a man's own nature we call it *vice*, in which view the moralist has to do with it; and when it injures a fellow-man or human society, we designate it as *crime*, which is dealt with by the legislator; so when viewed as an offence against God we describe it as *sin*, in which aspect it is considered by the theologian. But this distinction of the terms vice, crime, and sin, though convenient and common, is only of modern date. In ancient times we do not find the several ideas expressed by different words in each language, but rather one aspect of evil is almost exclusively predominant in the heathen world, and another where the light of revelation shone. In classical Greek and Latin, ἁμαρτία and *peccatum* had not that deep religious meaning that *sin* has for us; while the notion of κακία, *vitium*, was largely employed by the philosophic and moral writers.

In the Bible, sin much more commonly denotes an offence against God; but it is also used, often in the Old Testament and sometimes in the New Testament, for an offence against a fellow-man. The distinction that we make between *sin* and *crime* is expressed, not by different words, but by the mention of the persons offended, as in 1 Sam. ii. 25; Acts xxv. 8, 10, 11. The Greek words, ἀδικεῖν, ἀδίκημα, properly denote crime, but are sometimes used in the New Testament in a religious sense. The notion of vice very rarely occurs in the Bible, but it is expressed by *sin* (Prov. vi. 32; 1 Cor. vi. 18). The word vice never occurs in the English Bible, but once in the Apocrypha (Wisd. vii. 30) for κακία. But in the New Testament κακία denotes, not vice in the modern sense, but generally malice. Crime in the Authorised Version is used in the sense of *crimen*, accusation (Acts xxv. 16, 27), where the Revisers have altered it to "matters," "charges."

The primary meaning of the Hebrew and Greek words for sin, though not shedding very much light on the subject, bears out the view just given, so far as it goes. חטאת in Hebrew, and ἁμαρτία in Greek, seem both to have meant originally a missing of the mark; עָוֹן means literally crooked, as opposed to יָשָׁר, straight or upright, like our wrong (*i.e.* wrung), opposed to right (*rectus*). פֶּשַׁע, like the Greek παρακοή, is properly rebellion, disobedience; παράβασις is a stepping aside or across, *transgressio;* παράπτωμα, a falling aside. The etymology of the Latin *peccatum*, the English *sin*, and the German *Sünde* is obscure, and does not throw any light on the subject; but it may be noticed that Cicero says, " peccare est tanquam transilire lineas" (*Paradox.* iii.), and distinguishes *peccatum*, as the act, from *vitium*, the *pravitas animi*, from which it proceeds. (See on *vitium*, Tusc. *Quæst.* iv. 13.)

The general idea in all these words, where a derivation can be traced, is that of deviation from a line that ought to be followed, or disobedience to a command that ought to be obeyed. In many nations, indeed, men's thoughts did not rise above the idea of human law, or abstract moral principle as the rule, from which sin is a deviation; but when God revealed Himself as a living and holy Being, as He did to Israel, there could not fail to arise a deeper and truer idea of sin, and of the nature and sanctions of the moral law from which it is a deviation.

In fact, the specific notion of sin arises directly from that of the moral government of God, or the special way in which the Creator of the universe deals with His rational and free creatures. He governs them in a manner suited to their nature, not merely by what are called laws of nature, which are uniform sequences of changes, mechanical, chemical, or vital. In so far as we have a physical organism we are really subject to these laws, and God acts upon us through them, whether we know them and are willing to submit to them or not. But in so far as we are rational and moral agents, and can determine our actions, God governs us by making known to us through our conscience what is right, and giving us a feeling of obligation, and of His will and command that we should do it. He has made us rational and free just in order that His will may be done by us, not through blind constraint, as it is in the operation of natural laws, but intelligently and willingly. He would have our conduct determined, not by laws acting directly upon us, but by the representation of laws to our intellect and conscience, and the free response to them of our will. Such laws are what we call moral laws, and they have two characteristics distinguishing them from mere natural laws. One is that they involve the idea of duty or obligation, so that under moral law we have the feeling that we ought ; and the other is that they are fulfilled through the intervention of will, and leave open the possibility of disobedience. God, however, maintains His authority even when men disobey His law, both by the inward agency of conscience, which accuses, condemns, and torments the transgressor, so that he cannot be said to have escaped God's government even when he has disobeyed God's law ;[1] and also by the outward agency of Divine Providence, which controls all things, and secures that ultimately sin leads to inevitable suffering and destruction.

It is when we view morality as the command of God, and as the rule by which He governs His rational creatures, that we get a distinct idea of what is meant by sin. When morality is conceived merely as an ideal, an end, or the end, at which man may wisely aim, the perfection of his nature ; then the want or opposite of it can be regarded only as moral evil, vice, failure of the highest good, but not as an offence against Deity. If, on the other hand, the will of God is conceived as separate from morality, requiring certain acts of obedience as expressions of homage or tributes of praise, the refusal of these would be a personal offence, or rebellion against our Sovereign Lord, but would not necessarily have in itself the character of moral evil. It is when these two views are combined, and it is recognised that morality, or the highest ideal of human character, is the will

[1] "Cur tamen hos tu
Evasisse putes, quos diri conscia facti
Mens habet attonitos, et surdo verbere caedit,
Invisum quatiente animo tortore flagellum?"
    Juvenal, *Sat.* xiii. 192.

and command of God, that we have the full conception of sin, which is moral evil viewed as an offence against God because contrary to His moral law.

Since God's law is coextensive with the moral ideal of man, it appears that the notion of sin cannot be limited, as it is by certain theological schools, to voluntary disobedience to that law, but must include everything that is at variance with it, habits, inclinations, and impulses, as well as deliberate desires, words, and deeds. The Bible distinguishes between transgression, which is a narrower idea, and sin, which is more general; for while all transgression is doubtless sin, there may be sin that has not that special form; as the Psalmist speaks of having been shapen in iniquity and conceived in sin, and Paul describes indwelling sin as a tendency, or law, in his members, to which he did not consent, but made most earnest resistance. The problems presented by this form of sin will require more particular consideration further on, but it is well to notice at the outset the full extent of the subject with which we have to do.

The fact that God marks as sin every deviation from perfect morality, though at first sight it has a severe aspect, yet in reality shows the great regard that He has for the creatures whom He has made in His own image, the care He exercises over them, and His desire of the highest good for each one of them. For the true good is the highest happiness for man; and when God reveals to us the good in the form of a command addressed to each one of us, and is displeased when we come short of it; this means that He cares for each one, that He would have us to attain our highest end, and will not let us alone, if by any means we may be moved and encouraged to reach up to it. The moral law which God has given to man, and by means of which He exercises moral government, is, in its very unchanging severity of requirement, an expression of God's love to us, and desire for our highest good. It is, in fact, a teaching and education, by which He would show us the ideal for which we were created, and point us the way to attain it. It is not indeed the highest revelation of God's love, but it prepares the way for that; for if the law, even when broken, was a pedagogue to lead us to Christ, may it not much more have been such if it had been kept? It is a form of the kingdom of God, which according to our Lord's teaching is our highest good, that fellowship in which God's will is done out of love, and His favour enjoyed by men. The dispensation of law or moral government is not indeed the highest and ultimate form of the kingdom of God—that is only attained through the redemption of Christ; but it is a preparatory stage towards it, and, had man obeyed, would have been a rudimentary form of it. Sin, however, comes in as a disturbing element, and, as we shall see afterwards, may be described as an offence against God, because it really opposes and injures the kingdom of God, which is the chief end both of God and man.

The educative function of the moral law, as preparing for the kingdom of God, implies that it has been revealed to man in different ways and in different parts from time to time. The fullest and clearest exhibition of it is that given by Jesus Christ, not only in His teaching, but in His life as our example; but He solemnly declared His precepts to be meant not to subvert, but to confirm and complete those of the law and the prophets given to Israel, the fundamental principles of which were embodied in the ten words given at Sinai. These were summed up by our Lord in the two great commandments, also given in the Old Testament, and in the golden rule (Matt. vii. 12); and as these brief summaries show us how all moral duty flows from one principle, so the detailed exhortations and instructions of the prophets, wise men, and apostles, who spoke as they were moved by the Holy Spirit, show us how the principle is to be applied to the endlessly varied circumstances and relations of human life. All these are different kinds and degrees of revelation of moral law from without, God speaking to us by His servants, and in the last days by His Son. But the moral law is also revealed within; since even the Gentiles, who have not the law outwardly given, show the work of the law written in their hearts, and their consciences testify to its authority as a command, by accusing and even by excusing themselves (Rom. ii. 14, 15). This inward revelation of duty has also its various forms, being more or less complete, sometimes crude and undeveloped, and sometimes reasoned out into full and detailed systems of morals, as by Confucius, Buddha, Aristotle. While some sense of duty seems inseparable from man's nature, and so it may be truly said that the moral law was given to him at his creation; it is not necessary to suppose that he possessed at first, either by external revelation or by conscious moral sentiments, a complete code of ethics; it is enough if he had a knowledge and conviction of duty in those relations in which he had practically to act.

The moral law, in whatever way made known to men, is to be regarded, according to the scriptural view, as the command of God; and deviation from it, as thus regarded, is what we recognise as the essential meaning of sin.

CHAPTER II.

COMPARISON OF VIEWS OF OTHER RELIGIONS.

THE relation recognised between religion and morality is a thing that goes far to determine the entire character of the different faiths of mankind. The Christian view, which connects them inseparably, and marks this by judging all moral evil to be an offence against God, seems to those who have been brought up in it very simple and self-evident; yet there are great and widely received forms of thought to which it is strange; on the one hand, those in which religion is made to supersede or exclude morality; and, on the other hand, those in which morality is sought to be enforced without religion. The former recognise, indeed, offences against Heaven, but do not attach to them—nay, sometimes exclude from them—the notion of moral evil; the latter acknowledge moral evil, but deny that it can truly be called an offence against God.

In the most ancient religions, moral and religious duties are not clearly distinguished, for violations of merely positive and ceremonial laws were generally placed on a level with moral offences, and often were even more dreaded as provoking the wrath of the Deity. This appears, for example, in the Homeric poems, in which, when the question arises why a god is angry, it is suggested that it may be most likely for the neglect of vows or sacrifices.[1] Such, too, was the notion of the Eastern tribes whom the king of Assyria brought to Samaria (2 Kings xvii. 24-26); and the popular religion of Israel itself was considerably affected by similar ideas, though the prophets contended strenuously

---
[1] See *e.g. Iliad*, i. 65.

against them. Such ideas always tend to make the conception of sin indistinct, and to allow an undue predominance to the positive and ritual element over the moral and spiritual. Religious duties come to be regarded as mere arbitrary observances, and morality is either ignored, or, when studied and enforced, is dissociated from religion, as it came to be by the Greek philosophers.

But, while very generally among rude peoples there is a confusion of the moral and the positive elements in religion, leading, where not corrected, to the excessive preponderance of the latter; in some systems of belief we find, what is still worse, such ideas and principles as altogether exclude the moral element, especially the moral aspect of sin, preventing it from ever being recognised.

Such is the case in all the various forms of the Brahmanical religion and philosophy, which proceed upon the fundamental assumption of the emanation of the universe from Deity, or of all sensible existence being a mere illusion, having no reality. These conceptions make the notion of moral evil an impossibility; because if all that exists is but a form or emanation of the one real Being and source of all existence, nothing that is can be truly regarded as what ought not to be; evil of any kind can be only relative, an imperfection or fault in this or that thing considered separately, but when viewed in relation to the whole of things, only a part of the necessary evolution or manifestation of the Divine.

Hence, while in some of the Vedic hymns there is a certain partial recognition of moral evil, along with ceremonial defilement, in the later forms of Brahmanism, and in the popular religions of modern India, there is no room for the moral notion of sin at all. Thus these forms of belief not only dissociate morality from religion, as has been done in almost every primitive and pagan religion, but exclude the possibility of moral distinctions at all, and teach that they are entirely illusory. The disciple of these creeds conceives himself to be united to the

Deity, not by any moral or religious bond, but by such as are physical or metaphysical. In the more popular forms of this Pantheistic system, it is believed that, since all are materially derived from the gods, their union is maintained, and benefits secured, by observing the proper forms of ritual observance, as inculcated by the authorised priests. Whatever men's moral character or conduct may be, if they duly perform all the rites required in the worship of the Deity to whom they belong, they are safe; these rites work by a magical power, and are of the nature of charms or spells. But, for the educated and inquiring, Brahmanism has another form, esoteric and philosophical. The connection of the disciple with the Deity is metaphysical, and is to be realised by getting rid, as soon as possible, of all things material or earthly, avoiding merit as much as demerit; because as often as any one ends this life with either, he must enter another finite life, to be rewarded or punished, and both alike prevent that absorption in the Deity, which is the only perfect happiness.

Thus Brahmanism recognises evil as that which separates man from the Deity; but since the Deity is viewed, not as a Being of moral attributes, but either, in the popular mythology, as a multitude of mere nature-powers, or, in the esoteric philosophy, as the essence of all true being, what separates man from the Deity is, not immorality of any kind, but either neglect of magical rites of worship, or want of insight into the illusion of all finite existence. In either case, moral evil as such is not regarded as having any religious bearing at all; and since in Brahmanism religion is held the paramount matter, morality has come to be practically disregarded.

While the Pantheistic religions and philosophies exclude the notion of moral evil altogether, there are others which recognise it very energetically, but in a too material and therefore misleading way. Such are those of the dualistic kind. The great historical religion of this character is Mazdeism, the faith of the Avesta held by the ancient Persians and the modern Parsees. This would seem to have been derived from the ancient, pre-Vedic religion of the Aryans, who were the common ancestors of the tribes that peopled Media and Persia, and of those that descended into India. Both in language and in the form of many of their religious and mythological expressions, there is recognised by all scholars an affinity between the Hindoo Vedas and the Avesta. But a comparison of these sacred books shows an entire difference, and even opposition, in religious beliefs, the Hindoo so merging God in nature as to obliterate the distinction between good and evil, the Persian so emphasising the conflict between them as to run into Dualism.

This latter faith is associated with the name of Zoroaster (*Zarathustra*), who is mentioned, in what are acknowledged to be the earliest parts of the Avesta (the *Gathas*), in a way that makes it highly probable that he was an actual person, who introduced a reform in the ancient religion of his country. These hymns or sacred poems describe a conflict going on between the worshippers of the good Deity (*Ahura Mazda*) and those of the false gods (*daevas*[1]). No supernatural events are told in these poems, but Zoroaster is described as praying to Ahura Mazda for teaching, help, and blessing; receiving these from him, and imparting them to his disciples. The feelings ascribed to him vary from confidence to despondency, and again to hope, as would be the case in an actual religious conflict. There is in these songs a character of originality and truth.

Hence most scholars regard them as genuine records of a very old religious conflict;[2] but as to where and when it took place there is much uncertainty and difference of opinion. Zoroaster's name is connected with Ragha in Eastern Iran or Bactria, though some authorities think the place of his teaching was farther west,

---

[1] This word is radically the same as *deva*, which denotes the gods of Indian religion, and indicates their being regarded as evil beings by the reforming party, just as the Greek δαιμόνια became the demons or devils of Christendom.

[2] See "Translation of the Gathas" (*Sacred Books of the East*, vol. xxxi.), by L. S. Mills, Introduction, p. xxiii.

in Media. Since the *Gathas* describe the country as under a king Vistaspa, and since Bactria was no longer an independent kingdom after 1200 B.C., when it was conquered by Assyria ; if Zoroaster lived there it must have been before that date ; and an antiquity to that extent seems also necessary to account for the later development of the religion in the less ancient parts of the Avesta.[1] On the other hand, the Gathas seem to be, according to the best scholars, later than the Vedas ; but their date also is extremely uncertain, though apparently some time between 1500 and 900 B.C.[2] Zoroaster, then, may have lived somewhere about the time of Moses.

In what is considered by competent scholars the oldest part of the Avesta, there is a very remarkable account of a call of Zoroaster, very similar to that of the Hebrew prophets. The soul of the kine, or herds of the Iranian people, is introduced as lamenting to Ahura their sufferings from injustice and rapine. Ahura asks *Asha* (his righteous order personified) who has been appointed to take charge of them? the answer is, that no one has been found himself free from injustice. Then Zarathustra offers a plea for the suffering land and people, whereupon Ahura declares that he is appointed to be their deliverer. The soul of the kine laments that she has obtained but a feeble lord ; but Zarathustra accepts the charge, and prays Ahura for help and strength to carry out his great work.[3] Then follows a series of discourses and arguments, setting forth the principles and precepts of this religion, mingled with prayers and appeals to the Deity, and also with denunciations of a party opposing the doctrines thus taught.

These ancient records give us the idea of a preacher of righteousness and religion contending against worldly and ungodly men, somewhat after the manner of the prophets in Israel. So

---

[1] See Freeman Clarke, *Ten Great Religions*, i. pp. 180, 181 ; L. S. Mills. *l.c.*
[2] See Monier Williams, *Hinduism*, p. 16 ; Freeman Clarke, *l.c.* ; De la Saussaye, *Lehrbuch der Religionsgeschichte*, ii. 15.
[3] *Yasna*, xxix. ; *Sacred Books of the East*, vol. xxxi. p. 6. Compare Ragozin, *Media*, p. 100 (Story of the Nations Series).

far from following the Pantheistic tendency of Hindoo religion, this system was so intent on separating all evil from the good Lord (*Ahura Mazda*), that it ascribed it to a distinct and opposing principle. This implies a very energetic conception of the contrast between good and evil; but unhappily the contrast was not regarded as a purely ethical one, but as also to a large extent physical,[1] certain natural things and agents being considered to be in themselves evil. The *Vendidad* consists largely of laws of purification; and these have reference, not only to moral defilement, but to physical pollution. Whatever is connected with death, leads to death, or comes from death, is regarded as evil; while, on the other hand, fire, water, and earth are regarded as pure. Hence it is that the Parsees reckon it wrong either to bury or to burn the dead, because it is polluting the pure elements of earth or fire with evil.

This view of certain existing things as essentially evil made it necessary to assume an independent principle of evil, and from this necessity probably arose the mythological fables which are found to some extent in the Vendidad, but more largely in the *Bundahis*. This element in the Zoroastrian sacred books has been compared to the Biblical Genesis, and the other element to Leviticus.[2] The evil power in the Zend religion is not, indeed, represented as equal to Ahuramazda, but as limited in knowledge and wisdom, and so inferior in power, as to be destined to be finally overcome. In these respects, it has been truly pointed out, his attributes do not exceed what has been ascribed to Satan in Christian theology. But in one important respect the notion of Ahriman transcends any that the Bible permits, since he is regarded as having the power to create, and actually creating some real existences; and this seems to imply that he is not himself a creature. This is what is properly meant

---

[1] It has been called "the religion of the confused mixture of the spiritual and the natural," De la Saussaye, *l.c.* ii. 16.
[2] Pahlais Texts, translated by E. H. West (*Sacred Books of the East*, v.), Introduction, p. lxvii.

by Dualism, not that the power of evil is equal to that of good, but that there are two independent orgins to which the universe is to be traced, that which is good in it to one, and that which is evil to another. This necessarily implies that moral evil is the result, not of the will of beings created good though unstable, but of the nature of certain things created by an evil power; and consequently in the Parsee religion, while many moral duties are inculcated and vices condemned, yet some things that are quite involuntary and merely physical or technical defilements are treated as sins of the gravest kind. Thus the notion of sin, or that which offends God, is not distinguished as moral evil.

Another form of Dualism, which has exerted great and widespread influence over men's notions of sin, is the theory that matter has an eternal existence independent of the Deity, and is essentially evil, and the source of all the wrong and misery that are in the world. Since few of the ancient religions were able to rise to the idea of Creation in the proper sense of production out of nothing; the highest conception possible, for those who did not adopt the theory of emanation, was that of an intelligent power moulding and framing an independently existing matter. Such was the view held by many of the Greek philosophers. Now, since this matter was conceived as much as possible to be destitute of good qualities, which were all traced up to the Framer of the Universe, it was a natural suggestion that to the independently existing matter might be traced back all the evil that appears in the world as it now is. This would seem a way to solve the ever-perplexing problem of the origin of evil, and to vindicate the goodness of the maker of the world; though it can do this only at the cost of a materialising of the notion of sin, in a way that makes havoc of sound moral principles.

This tendency was checked in the better philosophers of Greece, such as Socrates, Plato, and Aristotle, by their strong ethical convictions, but it appeared when the notion of the essential evil of matter was combined with Oriental speculations, such as were rife about the time of the rise of Christianity. This combination was the germ of the various systems of Gnosticism, and the notion of an inherent evil in matter, with the ascetic morality that results from that, is what the apostles single out for condemnation in these incipient theories. The various modifications of this central idea in these Gnostic systems brought the austerities of the Hindoo fakirs, the discipline of the Buddhist monks, and the dualism of the Zoroastrians over to the Western world; and though the Christian teachers controverted, with zeal and success, the grosser forms of these theories, the subtle influences of their radical view of evil, to a large extent, tainted the life and thought of the Church, and led to misconceptions and distortions of the scriptural doctrines of sin.

But while the religious aspect of sin has not generally been denied or ignored in the oldest forms of religion, which has rather, as we have seen, tended to exalt the religious at the expense of the moral element; in various nations the moral sense in time led to a reaction against that, and moral and philosophical systems were formed, denying or ignoring the relation of moral evil to God, and viewing it solely as an offence against morality.

The earliest and most remarkable of these systems is Buddhism, which was a reaction against the Brahman religion, with its Pantheistic philosophy virtually annihilating all morality. Like Brahmanism, Buddhism sought deliverance from the evils of existence; but unlike the former system, it sought this, not by absorption in the divine being, to be attained either by the performance of religious duties and ceremonies, or by metaphysical and mystic speculation, but by the cessation of existence itself in *Nirvana*, or entire extinction. This is not to be attained in this life; but preparation may be made for it, and an inferior degree of deliverance reached, by the knowledge that existence is the cause of evil, and by ceasing from all desire and care for it. This knowledge was first attained by Buddha, and by it he became more powerful than all the gods of the Brahmans, even the greatest; for the existence of these is not denied, only they are reduced to mere finite spirits, and the system at bottom is atheistic. The discipline by which *Nirvana* is to be attained consists largely in the observance of moral precepts; and the morality embodied in them is of a singularly high character, inculcating self-sacrifice and universal love, even to enemies. It is, however, entirely severed from religious sanctions, and consequently virtue is to be followed, according to this system, not because man is under an obligation of duty to do so, but because by so doing he will escape from the delusion of self and the love of life, which are the sources of all misery in the world.

The obligation of the moral precepts in the Buddhist system rests, I think, on their being according to truth; and the reward connected with them is, that those who do them shall ultimately be freed from all ignorance, and enter the state of *Nirvana*. Here we have a body of ethical teaching, as pure and elevated as any outside the pale of revelation, with absolutely no recognition of a Deity or moral Governor of the Universe at all. Gautama's last charge to his disciples, just before his death, is said to have been: "O mendicants, thoroughly learn, and practise, and perfect, and spread abroad the law thought out and revealed by me, in order that this morality (purity) of mine may last long, and be perpetuated, for the good and happiness of the great multitudes, out of pity to the world, to the advantage and prosperity of gods and man" (Rhys David's *Buddhism*, p. 172). This purely disinterested end of practising virtue for the good and happiness of others may have been in the mind of the founder of the order, and the more elevated of its members; but with many, doubtless, the motive was simply the attainment of their own deliverance from suffering, in the way Buddhism offered to them. The form in which a novice applies for admission to the order is, "Have pity on me and let me be initiated, that I may escape from sorrow, and experience *Nirvana*" (*l.c.* p. 159). The higher aspects of this system can only be seen through an abstruse metaphysical theory of the universe; and as that can be understood by none but the thoughtful and wise, it could only succeed with the multitudes by transforming its original atheistic and purely ethical character into one of gross superstition and formality. In Brahmanism there was a religion divorced from morality; and Buddhism, by a reaction from that, went to the opposite extreme, and endeavoured to give men morality without religion.

A similar recoil from the polytheism of the Western nations, which was also disjoined from morality, may be found in the Greek and Roman philosophy, especially of the Stoic school. Without denying the deities worshipped by the people, the philosophers, in their dissertations on the chief good, and the way to attain it, ignored them, and discussed virtue and its relation to happiness, without taking into account any religious relations. Practically they viewed moral evil simply as against human nature, or against right reason and the fitness of things, but not as an offence against God; since their notion of Deity was either the immoral *demons* of the popular mythology, or the mere absolute First Cause of all, not the moral Governor of the Universe. Hence their morality was practically powerless. This is well brought out by the author of *Ecce Homo* (Preface to 5th ed. p. xi.): "Let us compare a disciple of Christ with a Stoic and reader of Seneca. They existed side by side at the end of the first century. Was their view of the obligations resting on them similar? It was totally different. The Stoic rules were without sanctions. If they were violated, what could be said to the offender? All that could be said was, '*Nempe hoc indocti*,' or '*Chrysippus non dicet idem.*' To which how easy to reply, 'I esteem Chrysippus, but on this point I differ from him.' To Christian *lapsi* it was said, 'You have renounced your baptism; you have denied your Master; you are cut off from the Church; the Judge will condemn you.'" Only I would remark, that this writer gives an inadequate explanation of the difference he so well signalises, when he ascribes it merely to the fact that Jesus founded a society, and that this is the secret of His power. But Gautama Buddha also founded a society,—the *sangha*, or order, is the most essential part of Buddhism,—but it has not given his morality the power over the hearts of men that Christianity has. No, the power of Christ does not lie merely in His founding a kingdom, but in this, that it is the kingdom of God; in His revealing God as re-establishing, by the mission and sacrifice of His Son, His reign in and over men; or, in other words, that He makes pure ethics truly religious, and religion truly ethical.

Another modern view on this subject deserves to be noticed.

Mr. John Fiske states the relation of his notion of sin to the Biblical one thus: "On the anthropomorphic hypothesis sin is an offence against a personal Deity, consisting in the disobedient transgression of some one of his revealed edicts, and calling for punishment either in the present or in a future life, unless reparation be made by repentance or sacrifice. Now the theory of the Cosmist is in substance quite identical with this, though expressd by means of very different verbal symbols. From the scientific point of view, sin is a wilful violation of a law of nature, or—to speak in terms of the theory of evolution—it is a course of thought or action wilfully pursued, which tends to throw the individual out of balance with his environment, and thus to detract from his physical or moral completeness of life."[1] This, however, is not the same, but essentially distinct from the Christian view; and even if it maintains a really moral view of sin, it is fatally defective by excluding the religious aspect of it. But it may be asked on what ground, "from the scientific point of view," does Mr. Fiske introduce the qualification "wilful" into his definition of sin? The consequences of a "violation of a law of nature" are not affected by the circumstance that it is voluntary; but follow, with equal certainty and effect, when it has happened through ignorance or inadvertence. If a man injures his health by overwork or sensual indulgence, disease or decrepitude follows, as surely if he has done so ignorantly or under compulsion as if he had acted wilfully. The only consequences of such actions that are affected by the difference of its being wilful or not, are

[1] *Cosmic Philosophy*, ii. p. 455.

the subjective ones. The effect on one's own feelings of a disregard of natural law is indeed very different, when it has been voluntary, from what it is when it has been unconscious or unintentional. In the latter case it is felt only as a misfortune, like a fall caused by a stumble in the dark; in the former case there is the feeling that it is one's own doing, and there is a sense of guilt, or folly, or self-sacrifice, according to what has been the motive of the action. Mr. Fiske was probably led to introduce into his definition the element of wilfulness, which has no influence on the physical consequences of disregarding a law of nature, because, without that element, the definition would have no moral character at all; but even the introduction of that qualification does not give it a truly moral character. For there may be, and often have been, cases in which a most deliberate disregard of a law of nature is not wrong, but in the highest degree moral and praiseworthy; as when Milton deliberately incurred blindness by the labour and study he gave to his defence of the liberty of the English people.

The fact is that the laws of nature, in terms of which this definition of sin is framed, are but declarations of facts, of what is; not of duty, or of what ought to be; and therefore they can only be the ground of a hypothetical imperative, not of a categorical one. They can only say, "If thou wouldest be healthy, and live long, and be happy, then observe the laws of health, and prudence, and social order;" but they cannot say absolutely, "Whatever thou wouldest or wouldest not, thou oughtest to live soberly, and righteously, and godly." This law, of which sin is the transgression, is of a totally different kind from the laws of nature, and any conception of sin that does not recognise this must be radically defective. Mr. Fiske recognises moral as well as physical completeness of life as secured by the individual man being in balance with his environment. If this is proved by the Cosmic philosophy, it implies that the power that is manifested in the universe tends towards the moral perfection of man; or, in the language of Matthew Arnold, is a power that makes for righteousness.

But we find it impossible to conceive of such a power being otherwise than personal and moral, that is, a mind analogous to our minds, that desires and seeks moral goodness in man, and makes the course of nature tend to encourage it; and we believe that the same power has also made man's nature such as to favour virtue, and impressed him with a sense of moral obligation to practise it. This power we believe to be God, and this sense of duty to be God's law written in the conscience or heart of man.

CHAPTER III.

EVIDENCE OF THE TRUTH OF THE BIBLICAL VIEW.

INDIRECTLY, the Christian view of moral evil as sin against God is supported by the fact that it is capable of being clearly and consistently explained, and that the objections that have been made against it can be refuted; but the direct and positive proof of it lies in an appeal to every man's own conscience as in the sight of God; on which his moral and religious nature will spontaneously recognise it as true. It may clear the way for such an appeal to exhibit the notion of sin as distinctly as possible, and to free it from misunderstandings and objections.

When we speak, then, of sin as an offence against God, we are not to suppose that it injures Him in the same sense as crime really hurts a man's neighbour, or the society in which he lives, and as vice really deteriorates and destroys his own nature. The almighty and ever-blessed Creator cannot be thus affected by any wrong-doing of ours. "If thou sinnest," says Elihu to Job (xxxv. 6), "what doest thou against Him? or if thy transgressions be multiplied, what doest thou unto Him?" For this reason, perhaps, Paul, when describing (Rom. i. 18-25) the impiety and ingratitude of men to God, adds, "who is blessed for ever."[1] Neither is it to be supposed that God asks for some homage or tribute from us, as due to Himself, and resents the withholding of it as a personal offence. That is contrary to the whole representations of Scripture. "I desired mercy and not sacrifice" (Hos. vi. 6). "He is not worshipped with men's hands, as though He needed any thing, seeing He giveth to all life, and breath, and all things"

---

[1] So Chrysostom *in loc.*

(Acts xvii. 25). The duty we owe to God is not a personal service over and above the fulfilment of the eternal law of morality, which is written in our consciences; nor is our failure in duty any personal loss or harm to Him. We must always take care, in all our statements about sin as an offence against God, to avoid any such ideas, for they inevitably lead to low and unworthy thoughts of God.

In what sense, then, can sin be regarded as an offence against God, since it does not and cannot lessen His perfect blessedness, or tarnish His unchangeable glory? The answer to this question is given by the notion of moral government, as the relation in which man stands to God. Sin is moral evil considered as a violation of the law of duty, which is not only made known to man by his own conscience as an abstract principle of right, but imposed upon him by God as a rule, enforced by His authority, and sanctioned by His government. As such it defeats and injures that kingdom of God, which is the end and aim of His moral government; it tends to prevent the realisation of that fellowship between God and His intelligent creatures, in which His will should be done and His favour enjoyed by them, so that they should be holy as conformed to His character, and happy as the objects of His complacency and approval. God earnestly desires this, and has expressed that desire in the most touching appeals, "Oh that thou hadst hearkened to my commandments! then had thy peace been as a river, and thy righteousness as the waves of the sea" (Isa. xlviii. 18; cf. Ps. lxxxi. 13). Sin is an offence against God, as the Representative and Guardian of the moral order of the universe; and hence it is defined by theologians as moral evil, viewed as a violation of the law of God. This is in accordance with the Scripture utterances, "Sin is deviation from the law" ($\dot{\eta}$ ἁμαρτία ἐστὶν ἡ ἀνομία, 1 John iii. 6); "By the law is the knowledge of sin" (Rom. iii. 20); "Where there is no law neither is there transgression" (*ib.* iv. 15); "Sin is not imputed when there is no law" (*ib.* v. 13). These statements make it plain that the notions of law and sin are correlative, and that it is in the light of God's moral law that evil is recognised as sin. In this light it is seen to be, not merely an injury to our own nature, as vice; not merely, it may be not at all, an offence against our fellows, or human society, as crime: it is an offence against God's moral government, and in all our explanations of its origin, and of the provision that is made for its removal, this aspect of it must be borne in mind.

Of the objections against the theological view of moral evil, as sin against God, many vanish at once on a clear and correct apprehension of what it really means; and of the rest none is more ingenious and plausible than that of Kant, founded on his doctrine of the autonomy of the will, which asserts that in truly virtuous action the will must be determined purely by reverence for the abstract form of law, as the categorical imperative, and not by any extraneous considerations whatever. But it has been generally thought that in this doctrine Kant was led, by his desire to exclude utilitarianism, to an extreme position, when he put regard to the will of God on the same level as regard to happiness; and the extreme rigour of his moral system in this respect has been felt as a blemish by such an earnest adherent of his philosophy as the poet Schiller, who endeavoured to remedy it by the introduction of the element of beauty, though Julius Müller has shown that it is in religion rather than in æsthetics that the true corrective is to be found.[1]

But while such explanations and arguments afford indirect and negative support to the theological view of sin by freeing it from obscurity or contradiction, the proper and positive evidence of its truth is to be found in the experimental conviction of the soul that deals honestly and frankly with its own state and feelings. This has seldom been described more truly and beautifully than by F. D. Maurice, in a passage of his *Theological Essays*, which Dr. Candlish, his theological opponent, thoroughly accepts and

---

[1] See Kant, *Metaphysics of Ethics;* Schiller, *Ueber Anmuth und Würde;* J. Müller, *Christliche Lehre von der Sünde*, i. 92-99; Dorner, *Glaubenslehre*, ii. 78.

approves. The summary and comment of the latter in his *Examination of Maurice's Theological Essays* will indicate the agreement so far of these exponents of opposite theologies : " The passage in which the entrance of this other conviction into the soul is described is one of rare eloquence—the eloquence of deep and true feeling. I am first confronted, face to face, with my own 'dark self.' Here am I, doing a wrong act, thinking a wrong thought, the wrong thought is mine ; 'evil lies, not in some accidents, but in me.' Then 'comes a sense of eternity, dark, unfathomable, hopeless.' 'That eternity stands face to face with me ; it looks like anything but a picture ; it presents itself to me as the hardest, driest reality. There are no *images* of torture and death. *What matter where, if I be still the same?* this question will be the torture, all death lies in that.' 'When once a man arrives at this conviction,' the author goes on to say, 'he is no more in the circle of outward acts, outward rules, outward punishments ; he is no more in the circle of tendencies, inclinations, habits, and the discipline which is appropriate to them. He has come unawares into a more inward circle, a very close, narrow, dismal one, in which he cannot rest, out of which he must emerge. This he can only do when he begins to say, I have sinned against some Being, not against society merely, not against my own nature merely, but against another to whom I was bound. And the emancipation will not be complete till he is able to say, giving the words their full and natural meaning, FATHER, I have sinned against Thee.'"[1]

It is, however, as Dr. Candlish goes on to show, the theology that recognises a real moral government of God by law and judgment, rather than the subjective and universalistic theology of the school of Maurice, that can best explain and deal with the conviction of sin. For, as already indicated, the notion of sin as an offence against God is clear and distinct only when God is viewed

---

[1] Maurice, *Theological Essays*, pp. 22, 23 ; Candlish, *Examination of Maurice's Theological Essays*, pp. 80, 81. The whole passage in Maurice should be read, and also the following paragraphs in the *Examination*.

as the moral Governor of the universe, ruling by laws which His intelligent creatures may disobey, in such a sense that they thereby grieve the heart of the God who is love, and frustrate that kingdom of God that is the end and aim of His counsels.

As a violation of the law of God, and tending to frustrate that kingdom which is the last end of God's works, moral evil is most really an offence against God, and as such it is represented to us in Scripture in various ways. It is often described as the object of God's hatred—it is that abominable thing which He hates, for He is of purer eyes than to behold evil, and cannot look on iniquity; it offends the eyes of His glory. This is the aspect in which evil appears in the light of the holiness of God. Again, it is frequently represented as displeasing, paining, grieving His spirit, and breaking His heart; and that in proportion to the degree in which His love is wilfully rejected, abused, or requited with ingratitude. This is the aspect in which it appears in the light of God's love.

These representations are scriptural, and are not to be explained away as mere figures of speech. God is indeed ever and perfectly blessed, and no action of the creature can ever really hurt Him in the way of diminishing any of His perfections. Yet as every evil action is a violation of that eternal law of goodness which God loves, and which is the transcript of His moral attributes, it is not only a wrong done against that law, but a hindrance or check to what God earnestly desires. And as among creatures it implies greater perfection to perceive and feel what is really wrong and evil than to be insensible and apathetic towards it, so it is consistent with, nay, required by, the infinite perfection of the Divine Being to feel real displeasure and sorrow at the sins of His rational creatures, made in His own image.[1]

In this view we can see the exceeding sinfulness, and truly infinite evil of sin, of sin as such, and therefore of all and every sin, as causing real displeasure and grief to the infinitely holy and loving God, and tending to frustrate the greatest, most worthy,

[1] See John Howe, *Living Temple*, Part II. ch. ii. § 6.

and most beneficent design conceivable, the kingdom of God. The endurance of the greatest amount of suffering is to be preferred to the commission of the least sin, so far does moral evil exceed what is only physical ; and though offences against men, or against society, when viewed only in these lights, are of limited and measurable gravity, yet wrong-doing, considered in relation to God, has no bounds to its hatefulness. For, as Dr. John Duncan said,[1] "all sin aims at deicide, and tends to the extinction of all being."

This view of sin as an infinite evil, because committed against God, is not a metaphysical subtlety, but a genuine moral judgment, and it enters deeply into the Christian view of religion. The absence of it is, in many cases, the reason why men do not see the need of the redemptive mission of Christ, or of anything more than natural religion. So Lord Herbert of Cherbury, the first of the English Deists, holding that a virtuous man may go securely through all the religions, says:[2] "This virtue, therefore, I shall recommend to my posterity as the greatest perfection he can attain unto in this life, and the pledge of eternal happiness hereafter ; there being none that can justly hope of an union with the supreme God, that doth not come as near to Him in this life in virtue and goodness as he can ; so that if human frailty do interrupt this union by committing faults that make him incapable of his everlasting happiness, it will be fit by a serious repentance to expiate and emaculate these faults, and for the rest trust to the mercy of God, his Creator, Redeemer, and Preserver, who, being our Father, and knowing well in what a weak condition through infirmities we are, will, I doubt not, commiserate these transgressions we commit, when they are done without desire to offend His Divine Majesty, and together rectify our understanding through His grace ; since we commonly sin through no other cause but that we mistook a true good for that which was only

---

[1] *Colloquia Peripatetica*, p. 14.
[2] *Life of Lord Herbert of Cherbury*, by himself, p. 49 (Cassell's National Library).

apparent, and so were deceived by making an undue election in the objects proposed to us, wherein, though it will be fit for every man to confess that he hath offended an infinite Majesty and Power, yet as upon better consideration he finds he did not mean infinitely to offend, there will be just reason to believe that God will not inflict an infinite punishment upon him if he be truly penitent, so that His justice may be satisfied, if not with man's repentance, yet at least with some temporal punishment here or hereafter, such as may be proportionable to the offence." Little wonder that with such an inadequate sense of the evil of sin, he did not see the need of Christianity as a redemption from it. Very different were the sentiments of his saintly brother, George Herbert, in his poem on the Agony—

> " Philosophers have measured mountains,
> Fathomed the depth of seas, of states, and kings,
> Walked with a staff to heaven, and traced fountains:
> But there are two vast, spacious things,
> The which to measure it doth more behove;
> Yet few there be that sound them: Sin and Love."
>
> *The Temple.*

CHAPTER IV.

THE NOTION OF GUILT CONNECTED WITH SIN.

THE Biblical view of moral evil explains and accounts for the guilt that is recognised and felt to follow it where the conscience is in a right state, and this affords a confirmation of the conception of sin as a deviation from the law of God's moral government.

The English word *guilt* is used by theologians in two senses, to represent two different Latin words, *culpa* and *reatus*. In its ordinary meaning, in general English literature, it denotes only the former, blameworthiness, culpability, criminality; but as the Latin word *reatus* expresses an idea closely akin to this, liability or obligation to suffer punishment, an idea for which there is no single word in English, and as this is an idea found in Scripture, which we have often occasion to use in theology, the word guilt has been employed for it as well as for the other. This use of the word may have been unwise, and it certainly has led sometimes to confusion and misunderstanding; but it can hardly be helped now, and we must endeavour to avoid mistakes by keeping the two meanings of the term distinct, as denoting two different though connected things that follow sin : guilt in the moral sense, *i.e.* blameworthiness or ill desert, *culpa;* and guilt in the legal sense, *i.e.* liability or obligation to punishment, *reatus*.

The former is inseparable from sin, and follows it as a deviation from the moral law simply as preceptive, apart altogether from its sanctions of reward or punishment. The sinner is to be blamed, as doing, or being, what he ought not. This implies that not only is the act or state morally wrong, and what ought

THE NOTION OF GUILT CONNECTED WITH SIN. 39

not to be, but also that it truly belongs to the guilty person, as the expression of his will or desire. If the wrong can be traced entirely away from the apparent doer of it; for example, if his limbs have been moved by a superior force constraining them, or if he intended to do, and believed he was doing, something quite different from what, under a mistake, he really did,—in all such cases there is no moral blameworthiness, because the evil in the action cannot be ascribed to the actual doer of it as its cause. This element in the notion of guilt in the moral sense is indicated by the terms αἰτία, αἴτιος, used in Greek to designate it, meaning originally causality, causing, and derivatively from that, guilt, guilty.

Shall we then infer from this that no blame or guilt attaches to anything but acts of will, or what is produced by such acts? Such is the opinion of many theologians, Pelagians, Socinians, and Roman Catholics, who hold that nothing but what is in the fullest sense voluntary is properly sinful or involves guilt. By Roman Catholics sin is generally defined as *factum, dictum, concupitum contra legem æternam* (Peter Dens); and Smalcius, a Socinian divine, defines it as *legis divinæ voluntaria transgressio* (see Jamieson, *Roma Racoviana*, etc., p. 97); this being one of the points on which these opposing systems agree. According to this view, an evil act, or word, or even desire, to which the will consents, is truly sinful; but the habit or inclination from which such acts proceed is not so, except in so far as it has been contracted by voluntary acts, or is yielded to by the will, and so is indirectly due to volition. If inborn or inherited, it may be called vice (*vitium*), and is admitted to be the material or fuel of sin (*fomes peccati*), but it is not regarded as properly sin, or blameworthy.

This theory has considerable plausibility, but it leads to consequences that are subversive of the moral judgments of conscience, as well as contrary to Scripture. We instinctively feel that we are to blame for things not done by an act of will, *e.g.* for the omission of some duty, even though it may be not deliberate and of purpose, but through negligence or forgetfulness. Conscience blames us for a disposition that is selfish, passionate, indolent, or evil in any way, even though such disposition may not have been acquired by our own voluntary action. If we were to regard inadvertent omission of duty and abiding dispositions to evil as free from blame, we would sanction a very lax and variable standard of duty.

The teaching of Scripture confirms this. The inclinations and dispositions of men, that lead them to sinful actions, are always represented as objects, not merely of pity, but of blame and condemnation. See, for instance, Jer. xiii. 23; Isa. xlviii. 4-8; John v. 42-44; 2 Pet. ii. 14; Matt. xii. 34, 36. When the Psalmist confesses that he was shapen in iniquity and conceived in sin (li. 5), and when Paul speaks of the sin that dwelt in him (Rom. vii. 13-25), it is not to excuse or lessen their sin and blameworthiness, but rather to enhance it. The law of God condemns and forbids all impure and covetous desires, not merely those that are voluntarily indulged; and requires not merely holy actions but a holy character. "Be ye holy;" "Be ye perfect;" "Be ye merciful" (Lev. xix. 2; Matt. v. 48; Luke vi. 36; 1 Pet. i. 15).

The Scripture warrants a more comprehensive definition of sin than those of Socinians and Romanists, who limit it to voluntary transgressions of law. John says, ἡ ἁμαρτία ἐστιν ἡ ἀνομία (1 Ep. iii. 4); and so Melanchthon defines it, *Defectus, vel inclinatio vel actio, pugnans cum legi Dei* (*Loci Communis*, p. 109); and Turrettin, *Inclinatio, actio, vel omissio pugnans,* etc. So, too, our Catechism, "*any* want of conformity to, or transgression of, the law of God." Paul distinguishes transgression (παράβασις), such as the sin of Adam, from sin (ἁμαρτία), which is a wider term, and may be ascribed to those who did not sin after the similitude of Adam's transgression (Rom. v. 14).

If it be asked, How it is consistent with the principle just stated —that blameworthiness implies that a person be the author of the evil for which he is blamed—to hold men blameworthy for inclinations that are antecedent to, and not produced by, any act of their will? the best way to answer seems to me to be to admit that if, in any case, an inclination to evil be such and so great as to overpower the reason and will, and impel a man irresistibly to acts that he absolutely hates, as is the case sometimes with physical cravings, or insane frenzy; then our moral sense would regard him as an object of pity only, and not of blame, for such acts; but that where there is no such physical or mental derangement, but the inclination is simply an inordinate desire for some gratification, the will is always active in it, and as it is on that very account an evil will, it cannot be exempt from blame. If the evil will has been stimulated by temptation, the tempter has a certain share in producing the result, and therefore a share of the blame; if a bias to evil has been inherited, and caused by the evil life of parents or ancestors, they in like manner have a share in the blame, and the moral guilt of the offender is judged to be less on these accounts. But it is not entirely removed as long as he is a rational and voluntary agent, for the inclination itself is a movement of the will; he has it not unwillingly. If a man has inherited a sensual, or a proud, or a passionate temper, we make some allowance for the greater difficulty he will have than others in conforming to the divine law; but still it is not against his will that he has it, and we must regard it as morally wrong and blamable.

Guilt, in this moral sense of the term, is inseparable from sin. As an act once done cannot be undone, so if it be morally evil, it can never cease to be true that it is to be condemned, and the doer of it is blameworthy. An inclination to evil may indeed be overcome or altered, and so the blame of it may cease for the future; but it will always be true that it has existed, and that it deserved blame. The ill-desert never can be transferred to any other than the person by whom an evil deed has been done, or to whom an evil inclination belongs. Others may suffer in consequence of our sin or sinful character, or may voluntarily undertake to relieve us of the outward consequences of them, but the moral guilt in the sight of God must ever be our own, none can separate that from sin in the eyes of the righteous Judge.

When theologians speak of a transference of guilt, or of an imputation of it to others than the sinner himself, they use the word guilt, not in this its proper moral sense (*culpa*), but in a legal sense expressed by the Latin *reatus*. *Reus* (from *res*) originally meant a party in a cause (*reos appello quorum res est*, Cicero, *de Oratore*, ii. 79), then the defendant, or accused party; then later, one condemned, and so liable to suffer the penalty of the law. *Reatus* accordingly means liability to punishment on account of sin.

This idea is frequently presented in Scripture. In our Lord's teaching we find the phrase ἔνοχος ἔσται (Matt. v. 21, 22, etc.; Mark iii. 29), where it is rightly rendered in Vulg. *reus erit*, in Authorised Version, "shall be in danger,"—an expression which meant then, not merely exposed to risk, but legally liable, as used, *e.g.*, by Shakespeare in "Merchant of Venice," "You stand within his danger, do you not?" in reference to the bond to Shylock. The word guilty is used for ἔνοχος in Authorised Version (Matt. xxvi. 66; Mark xiv. 64;[1] 1 Cor. xi. 27; Jas. ii. 10). In all places it would be better "liable." Jesus also uses the word debtor (ὀφειλέτης, Luke xiii. 4), and debts (ὀφειλήματα, Matt. vi. 12), for sinners and sins, viewed as liable to God's judgment; and He illustrates this by the parables of the debtors (Luke vii. and Matt. xviii.). What is remitted or taken away by God's mercy is not the culpability or moral guilt, but the liability to God's wrath and judgment, consequent on sin. See also Matt. xxiii. 16, 18, where he is a debtor (ὀφείλει) means he is bound. Besides these phrases, Paul uses ὑπόδικον γενέσθαι (Rom. iii. 19), to become guilty, *i.e.* under judgment or condemnation.

[1] In the report by Matthew and Mark of the Sanhedrin's sentence on Jesus, the Revisers have not been happy in changing the Authorised Version "guilty of death," to "worthy of death." The correct translation is that in the margin, "liable to death." It would seem that the Sanhedrin shrank from any expression of moral blame, and merely declared Him to have incurred the legal penalty of death.

In the Old Testament the idea is expressed by the verb אָשֵׁם, which means "to be desolate," "to be condemned," and is of frequent occurrence in the laws of sacrifices (Lev. iv., v.). As there used, it plainly denotes something different from having sinned; for not only do the two distinct words sometimes occur in the same clause, "he has sinned and is guilty," but there was a special kind of sacrifice provided to deal with the guilt of sin, the trespass-offering, denoted in Hebrew by the very name of guilt (אָשָׁם), and in the Revised Version more literally rendered "guilt-offering." The precise difference between the sin- and the guilt-offering is not very clear, but probably the former embodied mainly the idea of expiation, and the latter that of compensation. Anyhow, the distinct use of the words shows that in the Old, as well as in the New Testament, the idea of guilt, as implying an obligation or liability to punishment, is fully and clearly recognised.

Guilt, in this sense, is not inseparable from sin; since, if pardon is possible, the sinner, though he cannot cease to be blameworthy, may be forgiven, and thereby not merely exempted from punishment, perhaps indeed not exempted at all from the outward evils of punishment, yet freed from that displeasure and condemnation of God that forms the real curse of any punishment. This, indeed, cannot be done by God causelessly or lightly; it is effected only through the manifestation of God's righteousness in the obedience and sacrifice of Christ, and the sinner's becoming spiritually one with Christ by humble and penitent faith. The guilt that is thus removed from believers in Jesus by forgiveness is not moral blameworthiness, it has been expressed by theologians by the legal term *reatus*, *i.e.* condemnation or liability to punishment. This has been conceived by some too much in a legal way; but in the Bible, and by the best divines, the legal idea is transfigured into a truly religious one, which involves an element of mystery, but yet is most real. It is that which Paul describes when he says, "There is now no condemnation to them that are in Christ Jesus" (Rom. viii. 1). But this, according to

Paul's teaching, has been secured for us by Christ having redeemed us from the curse of the law, becoming a curse for us (Gal. iii. 13), *i.e.* becoming liable to the condemnation that our sin deserved. " Him who knew no sin God made to be sin for us, that we might be made the righteousness of God in Him (2 Cor. v. 21). This cannot mean that He was made sinful, or that moral blameworthiness was ascribed to Him; and it has been explained by theologians by the idea of the legal guilt, or liability to suffer for the sins of men, being laid upon Him by God, and willingly accepted by the Saviour Himself. This, therefore, is another instance of *reatus* being separated from sin; but the full consideration of these belong to another head of Christian doctrine.

CHAPTER V.

THE PUNISHMENT OF SIN.

IT may be convenient and proper to consider, in connection with the guilt of sin, what is the punishment to which that guilt makes it liable. For punishment is a notion correlative to those of guilt, sin, and law: it is suffering inflicted on account of sin for the vindication of law. What then is the punishment of sin in the moral government of God? Scripture speaks very often of this, and sets it before us mainly in two aspects, on the side of God and of man. On the side of God it speaks of His wrath (Rom. i. 18, etc.) and of His curse (Matt. xxv. 41; Gal. iii. 10); and on the side of man, of death. Let us examine the Biblical meaning of each of these.

The most positive expressions that we have as to what God does in vindication of His law and justice against transgressors are, that His wrath is kindled, burns, is revealed, against them; and that He pronounces a curse upon them. What are we to understand by these expressions? The words and phrases used in Scripture for the wrath of God are the same as those used of men, with this difference, that while in Old Testament this holds good without exception, and all the various words used of human wrath, even the most violent, are some time or other applied to the divine anger; in New Testament there are several words employed to describe human anger, and sometimes in Old Testament that of God, which are never ascribed to God by the New Testament writers.[1]

---

[1] Such are παροξυσμός used for קֶצֶף, Deut. xxix. 28, LXX.; παροργίζω used for רעם, Deut. xxx. 2, LXX.

In the New Testament there are just two words used indifferently of divine and human anger, θυμός and ὀργή, corresponding in general to the usual Hebrew words; though not used uniformly to translate these words respectively. The words are not precisely the same in meaning; but it can hardly be said that the difference is clearly marked or of importance in any Biblical passage ; θυμός denotes properly the inward feeling, or a passionate outburst of anger; ὀργή, the settled determination to avenge wrong; but these shades of meaning are not always intended.

The general result of an examination of the language of Scripture on this subject seems to be, that the inspired writers do not hesitate to use the words that describe anger in men when describing God's attitude towards sin, though in the New Testament at least they indicate that there are some forms and expressions of anger that are absolutely condemned in man, and not to be ascribed to God. Yet from the sense of the difference that must be recognised between the infinite and all-perfect God and frail and sinful human beings, theologians have found it difficult to form a worthy and adequate conception of the wrath of God, and have differed in their ways of explaining it. There have been three principal views.

I. That which arose from a great fear of ascribing human passions to God; and in order to maintain His absolute perfection, held that wrath in God means simply the infliction of punishment (ἐπίτασις τιμωρίας, Chrysostom ; *vindictæ effectus, non illius turbulentus affectus*, Augustine, *de Civ. Dei*, ix. 5, cf. xv. 25). This view may be traced back to Origen (*de Princ.* ii. 4. 4 ; *Contra Cels.* iv. 71. 2); but it prevailed throughout the patristic period with few exceptions, and has been countenanced in some degree by medieval and modern theologians. It rests upon the abstract conception of God merely as the Infinite, which would exclude all affections from His being, as inconsistent with absolute perfection ; but it forgets the other truth, that man is made in the image of God, and so fails to do justice to the representations of Scripture, especially to those in which the wrath of God is spoken of along with, and as distinct from, the infliction of punishment.

It is not fair, however, to ascribe the view, undoubtedly held by Origen and Augustine, to all those who have said that anger is ascribed to God by the figure of anthropopathy; for that only means that anger in God is not the same as in man, but does not necessarily imply that there is no emotion in God at all, as the Fathers just named hold.[1] Another thing that has led to the views of some being misunderstood is, that philosophers and theologians before Kant, by a defective psychology, recognised only two kinds of mental phenomena, knowing and willing, and included under the latter emotions as well as will and desire, so that when they describe God's wrath as *voluntas*, they do not mean to exclude feeling.

II. The view expressed by Turrettin is substantially that held by Tertullian and Lactantius in the ancient Church, by Melanchthon among the Reformers, and by many of the Protestant theologians. It is that anger in God is not a mere form of speech, but a reality, analogous to anger in man, though not identical with it, and, in particular, free from the sinful element that almost always mingles with human anger. Now, as anger in man, so far as it is right and justifiable, arises against wrong and injustice, and is an expression of righteous indignation; so the wrath of God has been explained as flowing from His attribute of justice, and by some, indeed, has been identified with it. Most of the seventeenth century theologians, indeed, have been over afraid of anthropopathy, and have approximated to the patristic view; but they have pointed out a way in which anger may be ascribed to God not as a mere figure of speech, yet without implying anything unworthy of God.[2]

[1] So Turrettin maintains, that anger is ascribed to God anthropopathically; but explains that by: "notat non ægritudinem aut conturbationem sed summan rei alicujus displicentiam et detestationem, cum certa et constanti voluntate eam puniendi" (*de Satisfactionis Christi Necessitate*, I. xx), thus recognising an inward feeling along with the purpose of punishment.

[2] See Tertullian, *Against Marcion;* Lactantius, *de Ira Dei;* Melanchthon,

III. A third view is that which regards anger in God as a form or modification of love. This has arisen in modern times among those who hold that God's character is pure benevolence, and the only purpose of punishment is the amendment of the offender. This view was adopted by Dippel in Germany,[1] and by Belsham and other Unitarians in England[2] in the latter half of last century; and similar opinions were held by Maurice, T. Erskine, Robertson, and others. A similar notion of the divine anger has, however, also been held by Martensen, a genuine Lutheran theologian far removed from the negative opinions of these schools. According to him, God's "anger is holy love itself when it feels itself stopped by the turning away of the being with whom it was minded to enter into fellowship." This, however, does not seem so worthy an explanation as that which traces it to justice, for it represents the divine anger under the analogy of a personal and even selfish emotion. And if we look to Scripture we find that the chastisement which God inflicts in love is not identified or associated with anger, but expressly opposed to it. "O Lord, correct me, but with judgment; not in Thine anger, lest Thou bring me to nothing" (Jer. x. 24; cf. Ps. vi. 1, xxxvii. 1). On the other hand, God's wrath is positively connected with His righteous judgment (Rom. ii. 5, iii. 5).

The second of these views of the anger of God seems therefore to be decidedly the most scriptural, and is open to no considerable objection. It is acknowledged by all judicious moralists, especially since Butler clearly showed it; indeed it was recognised long before by Plato when he made the irascible ($\theta\nu\mu\omega\epsilon\iota\delta\acute{\epsilon}\varsigma$) an essential part of human nature, that there is a kind of anger which is not a mere instinctive and almost animal passion, but a deliberate sentiment, that has for its proper object, not mere pain,

---

Loc. Com.; Amesius, Theol. Med. I. xii. 20; Turrettin, l.c. Others, as Owen (On Divine Justice, I. v.), De Moor, and Mastricht more nearly approach the former view.
[1] See Ritschl, Rechtf. i. 357.
[2] See Magee, Discourses on the Atonement.

but injustice and wrong, considered as morally evil, whether they affect us personally or not. This sentiment is one of the great supports of social order and morality among men; and when it is turned against one's own self it is the very scourge with which conscience lashes the guilty soul. It is therefore most natural to ascribe to God a sentiment analogous to this, and to understand it to be meant where the Bible speaks of His anger, wrath, indignation, etc.

As the sentiment of deliberate and righteous indignation is a main support of law and justice among men, and as the application of it by a man's own conscience to himself is the inward means by which the moral law is vindicated against transgressors, so it is an exceedingly natural conclusion, that the manifestation of this sentiment, in infinite perfection and absolute purity, in God Himself, forms the outward means by which the law is vindicated. "The wrath of God," says Paul, "is revealed from heaven against all ungodliness and unrighteousness of men" (Rom. i. 18). God's holy and righteous indignation is aroused by these moral evils, and goes forth against them. How then is it manifested? Paul indicates this in the succeeding context, when he says, thrice over, of the wicked, "God gave them up" ($\pi\alpha\rho\acute{\epsilon}\delta\omega\varkappa\epsilon$, vers. 24, 26, 28). He showed His wrath simply by leaving sinners to eat the fruit of their own sins. The necessary consequence of their ungodliness was, ever deeper, more shameful, and loathsome corruption; and this was the revelation of God's wrath against their sin. It needs nothing more to bring a just punishment on the head of sinners, but only that God should let them alone, and leave them to the consequences of their sin.

It is to be noticed, however, that punishment is not precisely the same as the natural consequence of sin. That may in point of fact be the punishment; but it is not simply in virtue of its following sin that it is so. There must be some act on the part of God, for punishment is suffering, not merely following sin, but inflicted on account of sin, for the vindication of justice. The act on the part of God may be merely a negative one, not a direct sending of evil, but simply a withdrawal of good, of Himself, who is the chief good, a leaving men to themselves, and to the consequences of their sin; still these consequences must have been appointed and intended by God to vindicate His law and justice, else they are not properly of the nature of punishment. Accordingly we find that in addition to the statements about the wrath of God, Jesus and His apostles use in regard to sinners various words implying an act of judgment; *e.g.* to suffer penalty (ζημιοῦσθαι), Matt. xvi. 26; accursed (κατηραμένοι), Matt. xxv. 41; chastisement (κόλασις), Matt. xxv. 46; retribution (δίκη, ἐκδίκησις), 2 Thess. i. 8, 9; 1 Pet. ii. 14; punishment (τιμωρία), Heb. x. 29; condemnation (κατακρίνεσθαι, κατάκριμα), Matt. xii. 57; Mark xvi. 16; Rom. v. 16, 18, etc.

Of these terms, the Westminster Standards have used especially one, *curse*, not perhaps the most happy choice, yet undoubtedly a scriptural expression. To curse is to pray against, or invoke the divine judgment, and it is used by the disciples of our Lord's sentence upon the barren fig-tree (Mark xi. 21). The noun "curse" is connected by Paul with the law (Gal. iii. 13, κατάρα τοῦ νόμου), and, as illustrated by the other parallel expressions, may be taken to mean condemnation, the divine sentence denouncing evil against transgressors. It thus indicates something additional to the wrath of God. That is His righteous indignation, as a holy Being, against moral evil: this is the solemn sentence which He pronounces against it as the King and Judge of all the earth. The punishment of sin, then, viewed on the side of God, is His wrath and curse, the revelation of His righteous judgment (Rom. ii. 5), the manifestation of His awful displeasure as the Holy One, and the infliction of His solemn sentence of condemnation as the righteous Judge. All the evils that men suffer in consequence of sin are of the nature of punishment, just in so far as in them God shows His wrath and inflicts His curse.

According to the representations of Scripture, this includes all kinds of evil and suffering. If we look through the word of God, we shall find almost every possible kind of ill, in one place or another, traced up to the wrath and curse of God. The sentences pronounced on our first parents (Gen. iii. 16-19) declare bodily pain, the exhaustion of toil, and bodily death, to be so; the punishments threatened as curses on Israel in the event of their disobedience (Lev. xxvi. 14-38; Deut. xxviii. 15-68), include poverty, sickness, famine, war, slavery, with all their attendant sufferings; and in the historical and prophetic books, all manner of evil, in body, mind, and outward estate, are represented as flowing from the wrath and curse of God. These evils are to a large extent the natural consequences of moral evil; and it may well be supposed that had there been no sin in the world, they would not have existed. Very many certainly, and possibly all, of the ills of life would have had no existence but for sin. This is a fact that observation and reflection can teach us; for we can trace most of the ills that flesh is heir to back to the evil passions, or depraved appetites, or ignorant folly of men.

But it is to be observed, that it is not the mere existence of such ills, nor yet their being the natural consequences of sin, that gives them the character of punishment, but their being ordained by God as an expression of His wrath, and inflicted in execution of His sentence of condemnation against sin. Apart from that, they might be calamities, or trials, or chastenings, but they would have no properly penal character, for the essence of punishment is, not that it be suffering of any particular kind or amount, but that it be inflicted on account of sin and for the vindication of justice. Any suffering that is appointed by God for that purpose is really and truly punishment; while the very same suffering, if not directed to that end, would not have that character. Hence it is that even after we are reconciled to God through Jesus Christ, and are no longer under His wrath and curse, we may still have to suffer many of the consequences of our sins. These painful consequences are penal as they fall on the ungodly; but to the child of God their aspect and effect is changed; for there is no longer to be seen in them the hand of an angry God, but that of a loving Father, chastening His children for their moral improvement, that they may be partakers of His holiness.

On the side of man, the punishment of sin is most frequently called death. This was the threatening to Adam in Paradise (Gen. ii. 17), this was the sanction of the law of Sinai (Deut. xxx. 15, 19), it is repeated in the prophet's assertion of God's righteous government (Ex. xviii. 4, etc.). Jesus speaks of death as that from which He came to save men (Matt. xvi. 25-27 ; John v. 25, etc.). Paul declares it to be the desert and wages of sin (Rom. i. 32, vi. 25).

That death in this connection means something else than the loss of bodily life, and worse than it, seems clear from the fact that in many places it is asserted of those who still have bodily life. This is done by Jesus (Matt. viii. 22 ; John v. 25, vi. 53); by Paul (Eph. ii. 1 ; 1 Tim. v. 6), and by John (Rev. iii. 1 ; 1 John iii. 13, etc.) ; and it is implied in the original threatening to Adam, compared with the account of what happened after his sin ; for we can hardly doubt that what did take place then was the beginning, at least, of the death that had been threatened, since otherwise God's word would be falsified. Adam did not lose his bodily life in the day he ate the forbidden fruit, but lived for many years after ; but he is described as no longer willing to meet with God, but afraid of His presence, with a guilty shame, and seeking to hide from Him. He still possessed animal life, for his organism was in correspondence with the physical environment, air, light, heat, food, etc. ; but his soul was no longer in correspondence with the spiritual environment, God ; he had become dead to God. In this state he had lost some of the highest and most precious powers of his soul, those of adoration, faith, prayer, and the like. Death therefore, in this point of view, is a negative evil, the loss of certain powers and faculties which should belong to man as God designed him to be.

In regard to the death of the body, the Biblical account of the creation of man does not represent him as endowed with physical immortality. The command in Gen. i. 28 to be fruitful, and multiply, and replenish the earth, implies that the individuals of the races were not to live for ever on this earth; and when the first man is described by Paul as being "of the earth earthy," and therefore corruptible and mortal (1 Cor. xv. 47), the reference is not to what Adam became by his sin, but to what he was as made by God of the dust of the earth. Scripture, therefore, as well as science, teaches that the human frame is in itself mortal, and not designed for eternal life in this world. How then are we to explain the statements which Paul also makes, that by man came death (1 Cor. xv. 21), and by one man sin entered into the world, and death by sin (Rom. v. 12)? Possibly the meaning is, that had there been no sin, men would have been translated, as Enoch is said to have been (Heb. xi. 5), so that, without passing through any disembodied state, they should at once have been clothed with spiritual and incorruptible bodies, such as we are taught to believe the glorified saints shall have. But a simpler explanation is also possible, that as Jesus and His apostles speak of believers as not really dying, but only falling asleep, when their earthly life ends, because they pass away, not in terror and despair, but in peace and hope; so but for sin, the inevitable end of man's bodily life would not have deserved to be called death. Sin may not have caused the mere physical fact of death to the body; but that horror and dismay with which it is so often accompanied, and which makes death seem the king of terrors, just as sin did not impose on man the necessity of labour and fatigue, but made these a curse.

The term death is also used in Scripture for the final doom to be inflicted on the impenitent at the day of judgment; and this is solemnly called in the Apocalypse (ii. 11, xx. 6, 14) "the second death." This is what theologians have called eternal death, though that phrase is not used in the Bible, and can only have been inferred from the fact that Jesus uses to express this awful doom the words "eternal fire" and "eternal punishment" (Matt. xxv. 41, 46). In that passage the substance of the condemning sentence seems to be, entire separation from God; and as God is the source and giver of all life, this may very appropriately be called death in the fullest and most absolute sense.

The passages in which this awful doom is spoken of by Christ and His apostles are very many and very solemn; and they are of two different kinds. In some, various images of suffering are presented, such as outer darkness, weeping and gnashing of teeth, the fire of Gehenna; while in others perdition, destruction, death, are spoken of. The former class of passages have led very many Christians to the conviction that everlasting penal suffering is the doom of the lost; but the latter have been thought, by not a few, to show rather that that doom issues at last in the extinction of conscious being. Clearly one or other of these two classes of passages must be understood figuratively; and the question just is, which? It is not possible to decide with confidence, and neither Jesus nor the apostles intended to satisfy our curiosity on this point. Even if the second death, which is the doom of the finally impenitent, entire cessation of life or conscious existence; this might properly be called an eternal punishment, since it is final, and its effects endure for ever. But although the doctrine of the everlasting conscious suffering of those who constantly persist in sin may not be so certain as it has appeared to most, the idea of the ultimate restoration of all intelligent creatures seems contrary to the most essential doctrines of Christianity.

CHAPTER VI.

THE UNIVERSALITY OF SIN IN MANKIND.

HITHERTO we have been considering the idea of sin, and have seen that the religion of the Bible gives a view of moral evil as an offence against God, which other religions present only in an imperfect or distorted manner, but which is recognised by the conscience and heart of man as true and all-important; and we have seen how this aspect of moral evil is based on the recognition of the moral law and moral government of God, and shows the infinite evil of sin, as involving guilt and deserving God's wrath and judgment as its punishment. But, unhappily, sin is not merely an idea, but a sad and awful reality; and we must now consider the fact of the sin of mankind, which is but too plainly made known to us by observation and experience, as well as by revelation. The Biblical doctrine in regard to the sin of the world, though it contains some things which unaided reason could not ascertain, yet, like all the great doctrines of Christianity, rests on a basis of facts, which can be proved and verified as most unquestionably true. The simplest and most obvious of these is, that all men without exception commit moral transgressions and failures, which the Bible and an enlightened conscience, as we have seen, judge as sins against God.

We cannot read the history of our race in the past, nor observe its character and conduct in the present, nor examine the state of our hearts and lives, without being convinced that mankind in general, and ourselves in particular, do habitually and constantly come very far short of the standard of moral excellence that conscience sets before us, and do at times very flagrantly transgress it. At least, no one who has any earnestness of moral conviction and feeling can avoid this conclusion. There are, indeed, many who have a very low standard of morality, or who do not think very seriously on the subject at all, who may fancy that such statements are the dark and exaggerated ideas of some extreme or ascetic moralists, and that the human race is not so universally culpable. Looking at the more open and offensive manifestations of evil, they conceive that these are comparatively few and exceptional, and that they are counterbalanced by a great number of good, kind, and generous actions. But every one who examines attentively the dictates of conscience, and the principles to which these may be reduced, and who has in any degree a worthy idea of what man's character ought to be, must feel that the doctrine of the universality of moral evil among men is true; and that, however it may be explained or accounted for, it is an undoubted fact, that, as far as we know, every ordinary member of the human race has, in some way or other, in greater or less degree, come short of the standard of moral character that reason and conscience compel us to set up as the rule of ethical judgment. There are, indeed, some details as to the origin, nature, and consequences of moral evil that Scripture alone can furnish; but the great general outline of the fact is plain enough, even in the twilight of nature's testimony; and the light that comes from heaven but makes more distinctly and particularly known what presents itself only as a less definite impression without it.

If we look (1) into our own hearts we shall find that conscience, which speaks with a voice of authority, and is sovereign in the soul *de jure*, never is completely so *de facto*. We fall short of our own ideal, and of what we know we ought to be. This is true of every seriously-minded man. There has never lived any member of our race, save only Jesus Christ, who has given evidence of moral sensibility and sincerity, and yet has professed himself to be morally perfect, or to come up to the ethical standard of duty. Any who, like the Pharisees, have made such professions, have been men who deemed morality to consist merely in outward behaviour, and observance of forms and ceremonies.

This judgment of conscience is confirmed by observation. For if we look (2) at the conduct of men, we meet with the same phenomenon. We know no man who is perfect, or free from moral shortcoming and blame. Even in the best and most admired of our race we observe defects and faults, while in many there are to be noted numerous and grave errors, vices, and crimes. The prevailing evil of human nature is proved by the very institutions and arrangements of society. The penal laws that have been found necessary in every state and society of men, for repressing the outbursts of passion and violence and the injustice of selfishness and fraud, bear witness to this; and the fact that notwithstanding the terrors of law and justice, crime is so frequent even in the most enlightened and best governed countries; the failure also, to so large an extent, of education and science, art and literature, philosophy and religion, to extirpate vice from among men, prove the same thing. Then consider the testimony of history. Are not its records just a continuous narrative of outrages and wrongs, of grasping ambition and insatiable avarice, of oppressive cruelty and fierce revenge, of bold injustice and secret fraud? How many pages does it unroll, in reading which we cannot sympathise with any of the actors in the scenes described! how few that we can peruse with unmingled satisfaction! Surely nature cries to us, from without and from within, from behind and from around us, that moral evil pervades mankind. This cannot be doubted by any earnest inquirer.

Consider, further, the moral shortcomings and faults of men, not only in their relation one towards another, but towards God. The light of nature not only shows the duties that we owe to our fellows, but reveals the great First Cause and Moral Governor of the world, and inculcates worship, reverence, and gratitude as due to Him above all. But how have men acquitted themselves of those duties to God? Instead of worshipping the one Infinite Lord of all, as a spirit, in a spiritual way, how widely and perpetually have they forgotten and dishonoured Him! How generally has religion been corrupted in all parts and ages of the world, when men have forgotten and neglected the one true God, of whom the whole frame of the universe bears witness, and deemed a multitude of inferior beings to be gods, the stars of the sky, or the forces of nature, or their own fellow-men, or the work of their own hands, even the rudest stocks and stones; and have worshipped them with foul and cruel rites, and ascribed to them attributes most dishonouring to God! Then, again, how much practical ungodliness has there always been in the world; and how many men, who have been just and good in their dealings with their fellowmen, have been utterly negligent of their duties to God!

The human race, taken as a whole, is one that is without God, or against God. In a religious, even more than in a moral view, the existence of evil is undeniable. The facts which I have briefly indicated might be drawn out at more length. But this is needless. They will not be denied by any.

Having considered the general fact of the universal prevalence of sin or moral evil among mankind, it may be well to examine a little more particularly its various kinds and forms, so as both to have a more distinct apprehension of its real nature, and to see that the assertion of its universality is not inconsistent with the fact that there are many and great differences of moral character among men. The universal sinfulness of the race does not at all imply that all men are alike in the nature and degree of their sin; and Scripture, as well as history and experience, shows that there are many different forms in which evil appears in mankind.

These may be distinguished by observing the various impulses in our nature from which sins proceed, and the modes in which they do so. Beginning with those that seem most simply and directly traceable to a single source, we find, first, a large number of sins resulting from inordinate appetites or desires. Many immoral acts (such as those of gluttony, drunkenness, unchastity) are just the inordinate indulgence of the sensuous appetites of our nature, and others are the result of excess in desires that are in themselves natural and innocent: the desire of pleasure leading to idleness and sloth, that of power to ambition, that of knowledge to curiosity, that of approbation and love to pride and vanity. All these desires, though differing in their positive moral value, are included in the term ἐπιθυμία, or concupiscence, as used by the Greek philosophers and in the New Testament, and all may lead to immoral acts if indulged in excess or in a perverse and improper way. This form of sin is the simplest, and the first sin of mankind is represented in Scripture as of this kind; it is that in which sin usually appears in childhood, and which prevails in uncivilised simple races, such as the natives of Africa and the South Sea Islands.

A second class of sins, very analogous to the former, spring from inordinate passions or affections, ill-will, revenge, hatred, springing from the excessive or wrongly directed exercise of the feelings of anger and indignation, that are essential and important parts of man's nature; envy from perverted emulation, jealousy from wounded love. These impulses are connected with what Plato called θυμός, and distinguished as a part of the soul, superior indeed to the desires (ἐπιθυμία), but, equally with them, needing to be directed and governed by the reason (νοῦς). This is the nobler and more heavenly of the two wild steeds that the charioteer reason has to guide and hold in. This class of sins is especially characteristic of youth. The second great sin described in the Bible, Cain's murder of Abel, is a sin of passion and violence; and such sins, along with those of sensual desire, are characteristic of savage tribes.

In both these forms of sin the evil lies, not in the desires or passions themselves that are the impulses to action, but in their disorder or excess; hence we must inquire further how it comes that they go to excess. Where there is moral blameworthiness, there must be possible a knowledge of the rule by which the desires and affections should be directed, and a power to regulate them according to it. Entire ignorance of the law of duty, or entire impotence to restrain desire or passion, would either of them exclude responsibility; but there is a conscience in man that tells him that excess is morally wrong, and he has the power, if he will use it, not only of controlling his outward acts by volition, but of restraining desires and passions by directing his attention to the moral law which condemns them. Sin emerges when such regulation of the desires and affections is not exercised, and the simplest form in which this takes place is through thoughtlessness or heedlessness. The mind which knows, or might know, the law of duty, does not remember it, consider it, and attend to it. See Isa. i. 3 ; Jer. viii. 7.

Such heedlessness will naturally lead to the indulgence both of inordinate desires and affections, according as either tendency may be stronger or weaker in particular persons, or as their circumstances may tend to draw forth one or other. These may therefore be regarded as subordinate varieties of the general class of sins of heedlessness, differing in the degree of their moral evil in proportion to the extent of the excess in each case, but all coming under the description of evil wrought by want of thought rather than by want of heart.

By such indulgence of desires and passions the power of self-control is lessened, and by the neglect to use the faculty of attention, so as to restrain the blind impulses of feeling, that faculty becomes less able to do so, even when it is wished that it should ; and thus arises the moral condition of weakness of will, when, even though the mind may be cognisant of the law of duty, yet some desire or affection may be so strong that the excessive indulgence of it cannot be resisted. These are distinctively sins of weakness, and they are specially apparent in the case of men who have been led by God's grace to strive earnestly after holiness in heart as well as in outward conduct, but who find that they cannot overcome tendencies to evil that are inherent in them. Such was the state of the disciples when Jesus said of them, "The spirit indeed is willing, but the flesh is weak;" and of those in regard to whom Paul so vividly describes the conflict of the flesh and the spirit. It makes no substantial difference whether the flesh is described as too weak to obey the behest of the spirit, or too strong to be controlled by it; these but express the same thing from different points of view. The accurate statement would be that the power to control the desires and affections by means of the direction of the attention is not strong enough to prevent their excessive or wrongly directed action.

But, besides sins that can be traced back to desires or affections heedlessly or weakly indulged, there are many that are quite deliberately committed, either without the knowledge or belief that they are sins, or in spite of that knowledge. Those of the former kind are cases of perverted moral judgment, when men consider something to be allowable, or even right, which is really wrong. An error of this kind, if honest, does indeed lessen the guilt of sin, affording an extenuation that ought ever to be borne in mind, and that distinguishes broadly sins of this kind from those committed against knowledge and light. Jesus recognises this in several emphatic sayings (John ix. 41, xv. 22, 24), which might even seem to deny any sin where there was blindness or lack of knowledge. But these are hypothetical statements, and may naturally be understood in a comparative sense. In His prayer on the cross for His murderers, our Lord states their ignorance in the strongest terms, not as showing that they were guiltless, for then they would not need forgiveness, but as a reason why they should be forgiven (Luke xxiii. 34). In like manner, Paul speaks of his persecution of the Christians as a thing done ignorantly in unbelief, but yet as making him the very chief of sinners (1 Tim. i. 13-15). The explanation is, that ignorance or error as to duty never can be entirely free from blame. There may be difficult questions as to the application of moral principles or precepts to complicated or obscure circumstances, but the essential difference between good and evil is plain to an honest, unsophisticated mind. When a man does what is morally wrong, believing it to be right, his error cannot be entirely innocent. It must arise from a want of careful attention to the nature of the action, or from allowing prejudice or self-interest to bias his judgment. Frequently when it is foreseen that a certain belief would make obligatory a course of action that is distasteful, there is an unwillingness to enter on or carry out an inquiry that would probably lead to that belief, or even an attempt by forcing attention on other considerations to prevent it.

Many sins, however, are committed with the full knowledge that they are morally wrong, and with more or less deliberate purpose. In this respect their guilt is greater than that of sins due either to heedlessness or deception, which is at bottom self-deception. But deliberate wrong-doing may spring from a greater variety of impulses than sins due to want of thought. It may be simply the wilful indulgence of those excessive desires or affections that so often prevail through heedlessness. Men may so far yield themselves to inordinate appetites, or desires, or passions, as to seek for, and deliberately embrace, occasions for their gratification; they may live for sensual pleasures, or for the pursuit of power, esteem, and applause, or for the satisfaction of envy, jealousy, revenge. This kind of conduct is described in Scripture as fulfilling the desires of the flesh and of the mind, walking in sin (Eph. ii. 1, 2), giving themselves over to lasciviousness (*ib.* iv. 10), running to excess of riot (1 Pet. iv. 3, 4), etc. This is the immorality of an age of enlightenment and civilisation, as sins of carelessness are those of a primitive savage state; hence there are more frequent references to it in the New Testament, written in the brilliant Augustan age of pagan culture and corruption, than in the Old Testament, which for the most part describes a society of comparatively rude simplicity. This form of sin is characteristic of full manhood, rather than of childhood or youth; it is most distinctively worldliness, the love of the world, against which John warns us, in the threefold form of the lust of the flesh, the lust of the eyes, and the pride of life.

But deliberate sins arise also from the selfish pursuit of the means of such indulgences as have just been described. The motive that leads to wrong-doing is very frequently, not the direct gratification of desire or passion and the enjoyment connected with that, but the procuring of the means by which such gratification can be obtained. Of these means the most universally applicable is money, and so, as Paul says, the love of money is a root of all evil; there is no form of indulgence for which wealth may not be made serviceable, and thus the pursuit of wealth lends itself to any one of those desires that are not of God, but of the world. In many cases, too, wealth, which is originally sought as a means of enjoyment of some kind or other, comes to be desired for its own sake, and even at the cost of all the enjoyments that could be purchased with it. Hence arises the unnatural vice of avarice, as seen in the miser who hoards money for the mere fancied pleasure of gloating over treasures that he never means to use. But short of this, and when money is still regarded as a means, the desire of it, even apart from the consideration of its ulterior ends, often tempts to injustice, fraud, and crime. In the class of means are also to be reckoned rank, knowledge, power, and reputation, though in the case of the two latter the desire of them for their own sakes is not unnatural, yet they are often pursued for the sake of the gratification of desires or affections. Sometimes, too, there may be several links in the chain of means that are sought with a view to ulterior ends; as a man may desire knowledge with a view to power, and that again in order to obtain wealth, in order to enjoyment; or another may seek wealth in order to knowledge, and that again in order to reputation.

Sins committed from such motives are those most properly to be designated sins of selfishness, because they arise from a deliberate desire of one's own enjoyment or aggrandisement, an excess or perversion of that prudent self-regard which, in itself, and in due form and measure, is allowable and innocent. In a wider sense, no doubt, all desires that lead to one's own gratification may be called selfish or self-regarding, but in the case of the direct indulgence of desires and appetites, it is the enjoyment as such, and not the circumstance that it is our own, that forms the motive to action ; and even in the case of consciously indulged desires, it is more correct to say that men are lovers of pleasure, or of excitement, or of revenge, as the case may be, than lovers of themselves. When they are deliberately seeking the means of gratifying such desires, then the element of self-regard is the principal one, and they are properly said to be selfish.

Still another source of sins deliberately committed is the desire to avoid inconveniences and evils to which the course of right may seem to lead. To this must be reckoned guilty acts proceeding from fear or want of fortitude, the yielding when suffering is threatened in case of refusal, acts like those of Peter denying his Lord in the hour of danger. These undoubtedly are due in a sense to self-regarding feelings, yet not in the same way as a positive desire of ease and pleasure ; and since they are committed under strong temptation, they must always be regarded as having a much less degree of moral evil than most other kinds of sin. They are frequently done reluctantly, against conscience indeed, but also against a real and earnest desire to do right, and in extreme cases they come very near to involuntary acts, though in other cases, no doubt, the fear that leads to sin may be but a base and selfish cowardice.

But the same motive of a desire to avoid unpleasant consequences may lead to sin in a much less excusable form, in cases where the consequences dreaded are the results of former sins. A man may be led to do a thing that gratifies no desire, immediate or prospective, that he has no pleasure in, but rather cordially dislikes, because it seems necessary to save him from certain dangers or evils that will otherwise come upon him. The typical instance of this kind of sin, is the conduct of Pilate in the trial and condemnation of Jesus, when he acted weakly, allowing his conscience and better impulses to be overborne by the clamours of the priests and people ; but that weakness was due to the fear that they would accuse him to Cæsar, and that he would not be able to justify himself for former misdeeds ; he was unwilling to run the risk of exposure and punishment for past crimes by acting justly now. To the same class belongs David's treachery to Uriah, and all the too common cases in which deceit is resorted to in order to hide faults.

But here it must be noted that moral wrong may often be done, not out of a regard to our own interests, but to those of others whom we are led to favour out of benevolent affection. To say that these, too, are due to selfishness, because we are seeking the indulgence of our own affections and find pleasure in this, seems an abuse of language; for there is no conceivable action that could not, in the same way, be resolved into selfishness; since even when we act out of a pure sense of duty, it may be said, and is said by moralists of the selfish school, that we do so for the sake of the satisfaction of having a good conscience. If there is any disinterested conduct at all, it must be maintained that when a man acts falsely, or dishonestly, or cruelly, out of partiality to a friend or relative, or from love of his country and desire for its welfare, he is not acting from selfish motives. He is impelled by affections that are benevolent, and therefore not wrong in themselves; but the evil is that in such cases the benevolence is unduly limited, and leads him to do wrong to others, which he should be kept from doing by benevolent affection for them also. No doubt there are cases in which love, or family affection, or party spirit, or patriotism, are largely of a selfish character; but undoubtedly crimes have been committed for the interests of a man's friends or country out of purely disinterested motives, and where this has not been due to mistaken notions of duty, it can only be explained as arising from a defective regard to the interests of those who are wronged—that is, from a want of benevolent affections to any outside a circle more or less contracted.

These varieties in the form of sin serve to show that it cannot be reduced to any one psychological principle, such as sensuality, as held by Schleiermacher and Rothe; or selfishness, as held by Müller and others. These theories require either that the application of sensuality or of selfishness be unnaturally extended till they lose their definite meaning, or that a far-fetched and strained explanation be given of some ethical phenomena. Sensuality, selfishness, and ignorance are real causes of certain kinds of sin, and, as such, they have a distinct meaning, because they indicate real impulses, leading to particular acts of immorality; but to say that Paul's persecution of the Christians was due to sensuality, or Judas' suicide to selfishness, is to give these terms so wide a generality as to lose all specific meaning.

Further, the sensuous appetites, and the regard for self, are natural, and not necessarily wrong motives; it is their excess or perversion that is immoral; the essence of sin therefore lies, not in either of them by itself and as such, but in its not being regulated by conscience; and as the power of conscience lies in the divine authority speaking through it, sin would ultimately be traceable to ungodliness, want of regard to God and His law. So Paul describes it (Rom. i. 19), and the temptation narrative in Gen. iii. seems to point to the same thing.

That theory, therefore, seems best supported which regards the essence of sin as negative or privative, the defect or absence of the fear and love of God, which is enjoined in the first great commandment of the law. Such godliness, in a simple child-like form, was natural to man as a rational creature; it would have given power to conscience to restrain the natural impulses of appetite and passion, but it could only be preserved by the attention being directed to God and His will as made known to man.

The view that moral evil is simply privative in its nature is not properly a doctrine of theology, but a philosophical theory. Even its most strenuous supporters have not asserted that it is expressly or directly taught in Scripture, and it has never been introduced into any Creed or Confession of Faith, and indeed only rarely even into systems of theology. Those who have maintained it have held it to be implied in other truths, and necessary in order to avoid regarding God as the author of sin. This was because they held a very high doctrine of Providence, asserting all things and events to be due directly to the divine working. With this conception of Providence, Samuel Rutherford said: "Allow sin to be an entity, and you destroy the notion of Deity." This is true, unless we lay more stress on the essential freedom of the will than the older divines did, or else modify the notion of Providence. So Dr. Hodge, who holds by the theory of determinism and yet rejects the privative view of sin, is not able to give any distinct account of Providence at all.

The theory is not free from difficulties and dangers, and is at best only a philosophical speculation; but as such it is not destitute of plausibility and interest. Most modern theologians regard it with disfavour; but they generally assert a freedom of man's will that the old Calvinists would not have allowed, and they have sometimes confused the Augustinian theory, that all sin is privation, with the position of Spinoza and others, that all privation or limitation of being is sin, which logically makes sin a necessity for every finite being, and tends to Pantheism. This is the danger to which both this theory of sin and the high doctrine of Providence, along with which it has been generally held, are exposed, though I believe the danger can be avoided.[1]

But whether the privative theory of sin can be maintained in all its extent or not, the analysis of the ways in which moral evil actually appears in human history and experience serves to show that they can all be accounted for by the absence of the fear and love of God, along with the desires and affections that belong to human nature. Now these are the very elements of which, according to Protestant theology, original sin consists. So, in the Augsburg Confession, Art. ii., it is defined as "the want of trust and fear of God, and concupiscence,' including in the latter term, not only lust or desire in the more limited sense, but all inordinate affections, and explaining that these are evil and sinful because of the absence of the love of God, without which the soul,

---

[1] See Dr. John Duncan's *Colloquia Peripatetica*, pp. 12-16; also Dr. James Walker's *Theology and Theologians of Scotland*, Lect. iii.

having no adequate object of desire, burns with inordinate love of earthly objects.[1]

Thus, not merely by considering the quantity of vices and crimes, but also by an examination of the various motives and impulses from which these spring, we may see that the actual moral history and state of mankind leads to the conclusion that human nature is somehow disordered.

But it may be asked, Does this necessarily point to any such moral catastrophe as the Fall of man, which Christian theologians have found in the Bible, or may it not be better explained in some other way? This question deserves careful consideration.

[1] See also *Apologia Conf. Aug.*

CHAPTER VII.

VARIOUS EXPLANATIONS OF THE UNIVERSALITY OF SIN.

THE universality of sin among mankind is a fact which calls for explanation, and most Christian theologians have explained it by the doctrine that human nature has been deranged, or, as it is generally expressed, depraved, by a transgression of the first parents of the race. Besides this, however, there are two other kinds of explanations which have been proposed as alternatives. One of these is that in some way or other sin is necessary, which implies that human nature, either in whole or in part, is essentially evil; and the other is that sin is due merely to the choice of men's will under the influence of example, custom, or temptation. Neither of those forms of opinion recognises any proper derangement in man, nor, consequently, any need of redemption; moral evil is to be got rid of, if at all, only by the necessary progress or evolution of mankind, according to the first class of theories, or by men's own efforts, aided by teaching and training, according to the second. Of the former class of theories there have been many different from one another, the most plausible and widely accepted being that which ascribes sin to the bodily nature of man, as constituting him a sensuous, and not a purely rational or spiritual being. This theory, however, shades off, on the one side, into purely dualistic ideas, such as those of the Zoroastrian religion, and of the Manicheans, and, on the other side, into metaphysical speculations, such as those of Spinoza and Hegel, that sin arises necessarily from the limitation of finite being, or the contrasts of individual life, as an inevitable stage in the development of man. We may consider more particularly the sensuous theory, because it appears to have some support from the statements of Scripture and the facts of the case.

The passages that seem to represent a part of human nature as inherently evil and the source of all sin, are those in which the flesh is spoken of as the principle and root of sin, and the carnal (σαρκικοί), or those who are in the flesh (ἐν σάρκι) or after the flesh (κατὰ σάρκα), are contrasted with the spiritual (πνευματικοί), who are in the Spirit, or in whom the Spirit is. This contrast has been understood by many to be simply that between the body and the soul, the animal and the rational parts of human nature; and hence it has been inferred that the New Testament writers, especially Paul, who presents this contrast most frequently, traced sin ultimately to the animal or sensuous element in man, as its cause. This explanation of the origin and prevalence of sin, the sensuous theory as it is called, has been very widely accepted on general grounds. We may consider briefly, first the question of Biblical interpretation, and then the more general aspects of the theory.

The word "flesh" in Scripture undoubtedly has a variety of meanings, though these are all connected and derived from a common root. Most literally it denotes the fleshy parts of the body, as distinct from bones, blood, etc. (so Luke xxiv. 39; Jas. v. 3). From that it comes to mean the body as a whole, as distinct from the soul (so Col. ii. 5). It differs from the word "body" (σῶμα) in this, that it denotes the substance of which the body is composed, whereas "body" denotes the organised form; and, on the other hand, it differs from the term "matter," as opposed to mind, because it denotes matter as living and constituting an integral part of human nature. But by a further extension of its meaning it is used in the Bible for man as a whole, including the soul as well as the body. This usage is not found in classical Greek, but is a Hebraism derived from the Old Testament. There the idea generally is the weakness and frailty of man as contrasted with the eternal and almighty power of God (so Isa. xxxi. 3, xl. 5, 6).

Now it has been generally thought that in the New Testament this meaning of flesh has been so far developed as to denote human nature as sinful, and opposed to the holiness of God; and this meaning, corrupt human nature, or the corruption of our nature, has been held to be the sense in which it is used when the flesh is described as the source of sin. This was the view current in the Protestant theology of the sixteenth and seventeenth centuries, and in substance it was correct. But its application was pushed by many too far. This interpretation of flesh was adopted in places where it is not natural, and the context rather points to the more literal significance; and even in places where there is good reason to take it in the widest sense, that was stretched to such a vagueness as broke all connection with the original meaning. But it is a much greater error to go to the opposite extreme, and maintain that flesh always denotes the sensuous or animal nature, and that Paul regarded this as the principle and root of sin. Apart from minute exegetical discussions, there are certain broad features of the apostle's teaching that cannot fairly be reconciled with that theory. One is that among the works and characteristics of the flesh he mentions things that have no connection with sensuality, such as enmities, strife, factions, party spirit (Gal. v. 20, 21), self-righteousness, spiritual pride (Phil. iii. 4–6). Another is Paul's emphatic teaching as to the sacredness of the body, and of all its natural functions and appetites (1 Cor. vi., vii., and elsewhere), so opposite to the ascetic morality that everywhere necessarily flows from the theory of the animal nature being essentially evil. Further, the apostle's statements in Rom. v. of sin having come into the world by the transgression of Adam, are directly contrary to the theory that it arises from the sensuous element in man; so that Pfleiderer, who holds this latter to be taught by Paul, is obliged to suppose that there is an unresolved contradiction in his different utterances on this subject, which is in the highest degree improbable in such a logical mind as that of Paul.[1]

[1] See Jonathan Edwards, *On Original Sin;* Julius Müller, *Christian*

The sensuous theory of the origination of sin from the bodily nature of man, if held absolutely, plainly implies a dualistic theory of the universe. For if the body be essentially evil it cannot have been created by the perfectly holy God, but must either be the creation of an evil being, like the Ahriman of the Parsee system, or consist of matter independent of and eternally coexisting with God, such as most of the Greek philosophers assumed. Both of these alternatives are inconsistent with the fundamental principles of Christianity and of Theism; the elaborate attempts of the Gnostics in the early ages of Christianity to bridge over by imaginary series of æons the distance between the First Cause and matter assumed to be evil, failed to satisfy the Christian conscience, and nothing of that sort is believable now. The crude and bare form of the sensuous theory may therefore be considered as obsolete, but views are still prevalent which trace sin to sensuality in connection with other speculations.

Although the animal nature may not be regarded as inherently evil, yet all sin may be ascribed to the preponderance of the animal over the rational; and a very plausible way of accounting for this preponderance is the fact that the animal nature is earlier developed. Schleiermacher held that in this way it gets the start of the rational powers, and that this accounts for the prevalence of sin in mankind. Similarly, evolutionist philosophers, carrying that theory to its fullest extent, and applying it to the mind as well as the body, hold that a state of savage rudeness in which moral evil prevails is a necessary stage in the development of the irrational animal into the moral and civilised man, and that what theologians call original sin is, from a scientific point of view, "the remains of the brute in man," as Mr. John Fiske calls it. This language, however, does injustice to the brutes; for they, though guided only by appetites, are not immoral, and do not act contrary to their nature; whereas men, indulging in gluttony,

Doctrine of Sin; Professor W. P. Dickson, Baird Lectures, *On the use of the terms flesh and spirit.*

drunkenness, and debauchery, and living a sensual life, give an unnatural predominance to the sensuous appetites, and sink below the level of the brutes.

But let us look at the facts, and see whether the earlier development of the animal appetites does really give them an undue proportion, and so in any degree account for the want of moral rectitude in man. In themselves, mere natural appetites do not tend to excess ; because, as they arise from real wants (as hunger from the want of food, etc.), they cease when these wants are satisfied. This is the natural check provided against their becoming excessive ; and this operates in animals, among whom there is no gluttony or drunkenness. In the early stage of human life, before self-consciousness has awakened, these animal appetites, as they are needful for the preservation of life, may in a normal condition be regulated in this way. What first tends to excess is not the animal appetite itself, but the desire of pleasure in the gratification of it. For a beneficent purpose, pleasure has been connected with the satisfaction of our natural appetites; but when this pleasure comes to be desired for its own sake, then the danger of excess comes in, for the desire of pleasure has no natural limit, but stretches out indefinitely, and can never be perfectly satisfied. It is from this, and not from the natural appetite itself, that excess arises. But such desire of pleasure, as distinct from the desire of what will satisfy the appetite, does not find place in the brute, nor in the infant as long as he has no more consciousness than a brute ; and by the natural provision, that makes every infant the object of parental love, as soon as the child is conscious of pleasure as a thing to be desired, he is also conscious of being the object of the most tender, self-sacrificing love, the love that of all human things is most like the love of God, a mother's love for her child. This, naturally evoking trust and obedience, should be a counterpoise to the selfish love of pleasure ; and thus the tendency that leads to excess in the indulgence of animal appetites has not really the start in point of time of a tendency to give heed to a loving training that would restrain that indulgence within the bounds of nature and right.

"The whole doctrine of evolution," says Leslie Stephen, "seems to imply that absolutely pernicious instincts are eliminated in the struggle for existence, and to fall in with the other assumption that virtue implies a certain organisation of the instincts, and not the extirpation of any existing instincts."[1] Yet he goes on to say that while every new sensibility or faculty is so far an advantage to the agent, yet it also exposes its possessor to fresh temptations, as well as gives him fresh capacities for virtue. This is proved by undoubted facts to which he refers. Hence he infers that in one sense effort is essential to merit.

This seems to show that free will must be recognised, and also that all the causes of men's immoral actions cannot be resolved into the remains of the brute, since most of them must be explained as due to the failure to regulate sensibilities that have been acquired later.

Observation and history bear out this view of the matter. In the childhood and youth of the individual, there are not such great vices as are often seen in later years; but neither do we see or expect such exercises of benevolence, self-control, or self-sacrifice as the mature man or woman often attains. There is not so great a distance between the goodness and the badness that can be exhibited by children as by grown men; both wickedness and virtue are on a smaller scale; their sins are not so heinous, nor are their virtues so heroic, as they may be later. The same thing has been noticed in comparing the characters of people in humble and obscure life with those called to take part in public affairs—

> "The threats of pain and ruin to despise,
> To scatter plenty o'er a smiling land,
> And read their history in a nation's eyes,
> Their lot forbade: nor circumscribed alone
>   Their growing virtues, but their crimes confined;
> Forbade to wade through slaughter to a throne,
> And shut the gates of mercy on mankind."

---

[1] *Science of Ethics*, p. 302.

The same thing may be noticed in the history of the race. In its earlier stages, the extremes of good and evil in human character are not so far apart; there are neither such admirable virtues nor such atrocious crimes as we see in more advanced conditions of society. Look at the state of the Hellenic race as described in the Homeric poems; the contrasts of character between Achilles and Paris, Andromache and Helen, are comparatively slight. Not much greater are the moral differences in the age of the Persian wars that separate Leonidas from Ephialtes, or Crœsus from Solon; but when we come further on we find a wider interval between Socrates and Alcibiades, and in a later age still we see men like Cato and Cicero contrasted with Catiline and Clodius; and then we may set a Tiberius or a Nero over against Epictetus and Marcus Aurelius. As time goes on the contrast still increases; in the Italy of the Renaissance we find Savonarola in the age of the Borgias and Medici; in France, Fenelon and Pascal under Louis XIV.; and in modern times we may compare such men as Howard and Wilberforce with Robespierre and Barère. The same thing appears in the literature of different ages; in the Greek tragedians and in Virgil the extremes of good and evil are greater than in Homer, but less than in Dante, with whom again they are less than in Shakespeare. It would seem, that as mankind has advanced from a rude and simple state of society to one that is more civilised and refined, while higher and nobler virtues have been exhibited by some, the vices of others have become more degrading and base, and their crimes more atrocious and detestable. The records of Scripture also bear this out; as the contrast, for example, between Saul and David is not so great as that between Ahab and Elijah, nor that again equal to that which separates Paul from Judas.

These facts, which are acknowledged by the most candid and judicious of the evolutionists, show that moral evil cannot be explained as a necessary incident in the transition from the brute to the civilised man; for in that case we should see that it tends to disappear as civilisation advances. But whether or not the whole or the average morality of mankind has been increasing as society has made progress in organisation, in mutual sympathy and regard; it is an undeniable fact, that this progress has opened possibilities of evil unknown in simpler ages, and that in a vast number of cases these possibilities have become actual immoralities, of increasingly darker hue, as the social progress has gone on. If it be held, as it is by Mr. John Fiske, that the advance of the race, under the law of evolution, is gradually working out a higher and more perfect morality, it must also be admitted, that while this may be so in general, or even possibly with the majority, the same process is also developing new and worse forms of immorality. And the appearance of these new forms of immorality is not due to the influence of the low state from which the process of moral evolution began, but must be ascribed to something that is equally operative at all stages of the process; and what would most easily explain it is what the old divines used to call the inherent vertibility of the will or choice of man.

This, at least, seems necessary to account for any deviation from the gradual progress of mankind from the rudeness of mere savage life to morality and virtue, which the theory of evolution would lead us to expect; but in order to explain the facts of human life and history as they actually are, even this is not enough. Moral evil has so universally a preponderance over good, that if we hold, as evolutionists do, that good is what is in accordance with the health and welfare of society, and as such should be gradually evolved by the survival of the fittest; we can hardly avoid the conclusion, that somehow or other the development has taken an abnormal course.

There seems to be, in the facts which all profound Ethics must recognise, reason to think, that there is something abnormal in human nature as it exists at present; its workings and tendencies are not in accordance with reason and prudence, and there is no certainty, on grounds of mere science, that the progress of a race as a whole will be towards moral harmony and goodness. Hear how Mr. Leslie Stephen speaks: "The savage deviates less frequently than the civilised man from the code recognised in each case. The savage law is lower, but it is more regularly observed. So if we go back to the animals, in whom morality proper does not exist, the obedience to instinct is more regular still. Sin comes through the law, as it is only when the agent is capable of laying down general rules that he begins to be sensible of deviations from them. . . . From the scientific point of view we may hold that evolution implies progress—at any rate, to a point beyond our present achievements, and, further, progress implies a solution of many discords, and an extirpation of many evils; but I can at least see no reason for supposing that it implies the extirpation of evil in general, or the definitive substitution of harmony for discord." [1]

To most of those who believe in God as the personal and moral First Cause of the universe, such a view of the state and prospects of mankind has seemed to imply some moral disorder of human nature; and in order to avoid this some have taken on very scanty grounds a far more optimistic view of humanity; but even if the actual prevalence of evil could be explained consistently with Theism as inevitable on account of the freedom of man, this would make it very credible that a God of infinite pity and mercy would, if it were possible, interpose in some way over and above the ordinary processes of nature to raise mankind out of such a state.

But while we cannot accept any view that makes sin a necessity, on the other hand no theory that regards man's nature as perfectly pure and uncorrupted can be considered as a satisfactory explanation of the fact of the universal prevalence of sin. Such a view was held by Pelagius and his followers in the ancient Church, and by Socinians and Rationalists in modern times. According to their opinion, all men are born free from any bias to sin, in a state of indifference or equilibrium between good and evil, and their character is determined entirely by the choice

[1] *Science of Ethics*, pp. 445, 446.

of their own will, under the motives presented to them from without. The keeping of God's law is possible to all, and indeed, Pelagius held, has been attained by some; but the prevalence of sin is due to the freedom of will in each individual, and the influence of the bad example early set by the parents of the race, and imitated age after age by their descendants. Undoubtedly, these are real causes of sin, so far as they go. Many evil actions and even dispositions can be traced to wrong choices of the will; and the tendency in children to imitate the faults of their parents is real and strong, and, having been in constant exercise for countless ages, must have produced a great amount of evil.

But can these things account for the whole of the facts presented by observation and testified by Scripture? The great majority of Christians have thought that they cannot. Evil dispositions are too universal to be explained in any such way. If that theory were true, we should expect to find that a certain number of men would have chosen good, and, giving on the whole a good example and education to their children, would have caused considerable exceptions to the prevalence of sin. But there are no such exceptions. Godly men, indeed, there have ever been, but they have never been sinless; and the more earnest and godly they have been, the more distinctly have they acknowledged that they are sinful, and that their goodness is due, not to their own nature, but to the grace of God. Even those who have been brought up most carefully by godly parents, and surrounded from their infancy with good examples, all without exception turn out to be sinners, and do not start in the moral race from the point of attainment which their parents had reached by a life of Christian faith and self-denial, but have to begin, like all others, by repentance, reconciliation to God, and denial of selfish and worldly lusts.

Again, sin begins too early in human life to be the result merely of education or example. Long before children can perceive or understand the example of their parents, they show the beginnings of evil passions, such as greed, selfishness, anger, vanity, pride, and the like. These faults appear in childish forms very early indeed, and need to be corrected, that they may not grow to more serious vices. The ease with which a child may be spoiled, even in the very tenderest age, simply by being let alone, and the need of correction from the very first in order to form a good character, show that sin exists in every one of us too early to be accounted for by imitation.

Besides, it is an unquestionable fact that parents do affect the character of their children, not only by example and training, but by the transmission of hereditary qualities. In regard to physical features and peculiarities this is undoubted; and the general law, that like begets like, is not limited to qualities of body, but extends to those of mind and soul as well. Mental power, and the particular kind of that power, whether a retentive memory, or a keen intellect, or a lively fancy, are frequently observed to be inherited by children from their parents; and so also are moral qualities, such as openness or reserve, firmness or pliability, coolness or warmth of passion. So it happens that different races have moral characters not less distinctive than their physical features. These phenomena are indeed among the most difficult problems that science has to explain, yet they are among the most familiar objects that experience presents to our view. In the face of them, it is impossible to limit the influences, by which man's moral character is formed, to example alone; and to account for the prevailing sinfulness of the race simply by men having been led by the tendency to imitation to follow the steps of their first parents in apostasy from God.

This view of human nature pervades the whole thought and literature of the great Chinese race, and has done so for ages, being embodied in the teaching of Confucius, and other sages of that country. The primitive religion of China in some respects seems to deviate less from the true idea of God and His relation to the world than that of most heathen nations. It was not pantheistic like Brahmanism in India, nor an unethical polytheism like those of the Western nations, nor sensuous nature-worship like that of the Semitic tribes, nor yet dualistic like that of the Persians, but seems to have recognised a personal Deity as moral governor of men. In the earliest of their books, which go back to about 2000 B.C., there is frequent reference to a Supreme Being, generally called Heaven, sometimes God, represented as protecting the righteous and punishing the wicked in this life; prayers and sacrifices were offered to him, but also to spirits of heaven and earth, to ancestors, and other objects of worship. The will of Heaven was thought to be learned from providence, from the teaching of sages, and also in some cases from divination. Morality was considered mainly as consisting in conduct, and human nature was viewed as entirely good.

Confucius turned aside the mind of China from religious thought and inquiry to morality. Feeling that he had no certain knowledge about God and a future life, he frankly confessed this, and did not profess to be able to teach men on these subjects; but he did teach men's duty one to another, and sought by instruction in this to reform prevailing abuses and elevate the people. He thought that men's character would be reformed by cultivating carefully the principles of their nature, and exercising them on the rule of reciprocity, *i.e.* "What you do not like when done to yourself, do not do to others."

Like the Greek philosophers, especially of the Peripatetic and Stoic schools, Confucius and Mencius, who came after him, showed that virtue consists in following right reason, and acting according to nature; and their arguments on that point are not to be despised. But they went on from this to the assumption, that if only men were enlightened and rightly instructed, and had good examples set before them, they would be made good, especially if kings and magistrates showed a good example to those under them. It is noteworthy that Confucius did not profess to have himself attained perfection; and even his ideal of "the superior man" does not include absolute sinlessness, but only sincerity in striving after it, acknowledging shortcomings when they occur, and endeavouring to amend them. In this we may observe a curious parallel to the rationalist notion, that a sincere though imperfect morality is all that can be required of men. The tendency of this teaching was to substitute a superficial code of external observances for real heart morality; and the whole history of China has shown that, though education and instruction are powers for good in their own place, they cannot overcome the tendency to evil in the soul of man, or produce real virtue.

CHAPTER VIII.

THE BIBLICAL DOCTRINE OF THE FALL OF MAN.

THE scriptural doctrine of human nature is the mean between the two extreme views we have been considering. It is, that human nature is essentially good, but totally corrupted. This view is implied in what the Bible teaches about the Fall; which is, that God made man upright, free, and able by obedience to retain his innocence and happiness; but that man, by disobedience, forfeited these blessings, and became sinful and prone to evil. This is the essential meaning of the narrative in Gen. iii., which is presupposed in the whole course of revelation, and distinctly referred to by our Lord and His apostles. That narrative is not, indeed, so often alluded to in the Old Testament as might have been expected; and the reason of this probably is that, under the Jewish dispensation, men's thoughts did not habitually go further back than to Abraham, the father of the chosen seed;[1] but there are, at least, possible references to it in Hos. vi. 7; Job xxxi. 33; Ezek. xxxiii. 13-16; and the general truth implied in it is asserted in Eccles. vii. 29. There can therefore be no doubt that when the Old Testament writers speak of the universal and inborn sinfulness of men, they ascribed this, so far as they thought on the problem at all, not to God having made them so, but to the parents of the race having transgressed God's command. This is confirmed by the facts that Jesus calls the devil a liar and a murderer from the beginning (John viii. 44), in reference to the tempter enticing our first parents to sin, and so bringing on death; and that Paul (Rom. v. 12-19; 2 Cor. xi. 3;

[1] See Dorner, *Glaubenslehre*, sec. 78.

1 Tim. ii. 14) and John (Rev. xii. 9, xx. 2 ; 1 John iii. 8-12) make repeated reference to the narrative in Genesis.

In view of the use thus made of it, that narrative cannot be regarded as a mere myth, or as a moral apologue designed simply to show how men in general are tempted and fall into sin ; it was evidently intended, and was understood by Christ and His apostles, to relate one momentous occurrence that took place at the beginning of human history, and has affected all its subsequent course. This does not, however, imply that it was meant to be understood as, in all its parts, a literal narrative; nor is this probable. The anthropomorphic representation of God walking in the garden in the cool of the day, must be regarded as figurative ; and several other things in the story, such as the garden of God, the tree of life, the serpent, are used as symbols in other parts of Scripture, and may be so meant here. How far precisely a figurative element enters into the passage, it is neither possible nor needful to determine.

The main point is, that our first parents, though created innocent and upright, were inexperienced and unstable, and had to learn obedience, as even the Son of God did (Heb. v. 8), if not by suffering, at least by self-denial. They were commanded to abstain from a particular gratification, and thus were exposed to trial, and to temptation to disobey. But this very trial, had it been withstood, would have raised their mere negative innocence to positive and deliberate choice of good, and given them, instead of their original unstable uprightness, a tried and confirmed character of holiness. So far as we can see, if man was to be dealt with as a free agent, by means of moral government, a trial just such as this must form part of his moral education, and was the appropriate means of his rising to a higher degree of goodness.

But it necessarily involved also the possibility of his falling by disobedience ; and this, alas ! is what has actually taken place. The way in which this happened is described in a manner very true to the universal principles of human nature. The first sin is ascribed to a threefold motive, the desire of sensuous pleasure, of knowledge, and of elevation to likeness to God, corresponding very nearly to John's description of the evil in the world, "the lust of the flesh, the lust of the eyes, and the vainglory of life" (1 John ii. 16). But the essence of the sin was, that these desires were not kept in check by regard to the word of God; and thus the real cause of the Fall was unbelief and insubordination; unbelief, in not giving credit to God's testimony warning them of death; and insubordination, in not submitting to the will of God. To this they are described as having been led by the deceit and temptation of the serpent; and this tempter is afterwards identified with the devil or Satan.

The Biblical teaching about the evil from which Christ came to redeem us, has been believed by most Christians to include the assertion of a personal evil spirit or tempter, called Satan, *i.e.* the adversary, the devil, *i.e.* the accuser or slanderer,[1] the evil one, the prince of this world. This belief seems to be well founded, because in the teaching of Jesus Himself there are numerous and explicit statements that point to the existence of such a being. To the allegation that He cast out demons by Beelzebub, the prince of the demons, He replied in such a way as to imply that Satan really had a kingdom, and that He had conquered him, and was therefore able to deliver his captives (Matt. xii. 25-29; Mark iii. 23-27). In the explanation of the parable of the Sower, given to His disciples apart, He said that Satan took away the word from those represented by the wayside (Matt. xiii. 19; Mark iv. 15; Luke viii. 12); and in explaining the parable of the Tares, He said that they are the children of the wicked one, and that the enemy that sowed them is the devil (Matt. xiii. 39). In the solemn description of the great judgment, He speaks of

[1] It must be observed that wherever "devils" are spoken of in the plural, the word is a different one, having no connection with the devil (ὁ διάβολος). The evil spirits that are described as possessing men are demons (δαιμόνια); and though Satan is apparently identified with the prince of the demons, that seems only to mean that all that is hostile and hurtful to men is under him as its head.

the eternal fire prepared for the devil and his angels (Matt. xxv. 41); and there is strong reason to believe that the last petition in the Lord's Prayer should be, "deliver us from the evil one." Luke records two other instances of His speaking to His disciples of Satan as the adversary and tempter (Luke x. 18, 19, xxii. 31); and John reports Him as speaking to the Jews of the devil as the father of lies (John viii. 38-44), and twice over, in His last discourse with the apostles, calling him the prince of this world (xiv. 31, xvi. 11).

These statements cannot naturally be interpreted as merely figurative descriptions of the power of evil or temptation; for although some particulars in them are not meant to be taken literally, the idea of personality is so distinct and uniform in them all, that it would be putting a violent strain on the language to take it as a figure of speech. As little can we suppose that Jesus employed such language merely in accommodation to the popular ideas of the time. He is not, indeed, to be held to have sanctioned all the current beliefs to which He refers, as, that the prince of the demons is Beelzebub, or that the Jewish exorcists cast out demons; but when we find Him speaking of Satan privately to His disciples, and in the explanation of parables, when no condescension to popular notions was at all necessary, we cannot suppose that He did not express His own belief. The occasions, too, on which such sayings are ascribed to Him are so many, and the sayings themselves so various, given by all the four evangelists, that there is no possibility of supposing that He was misunderstood by His hearers, or by those who reported His teaching. If our accounts of the teaching of Jesus are reliable at all, we seem shut up to the conclusion, that He did speak, with great solemnity, of a personal evil spirit as the great enemy of God and man.

Now this is not a matter of mere science or history, on which we might possibly suppose Jesus to have shared the imperfect knowledge of the time, without derogating from His authority as a teacher of religion. It is presented by Him as a moral and religious truth, having important practical bearings on our life and conduct. If, therefore, we take Jesus as our supreme religious guide, we must, I think, accept this as part of His teaching.

There is no reason to reject the New Testament teaching about Satan as inconsistent with science or philosophy. Plainly it relates to a region that lies beyond the range of scientific knowledge altogether, for that is limited to the world of sense and experience ; and whether or not there are living creatures outside of our world, and if so, what are their characters and powers, are questions that no science can answer, and on which one view is just as possible as another, so far as science is concerned. It may, indeed, be objected that many of the things that were formerly ascribed to evil spirits have been proved by science to be the effect of natural causes, and that no room is left by modern discoveries for the operation of superhuman spirits on human affairs. But this only proves that some of the notions connected with the belief of a great spiritual enemy were baseless superstitions ; and it would be rash to say that, on the mind of man at least, no superhuman agency is possible.

Any solid objection to the doctrine of a personal spirit of evil must rest on the ground that the conception is impossible, because involving incompatible elements or contradicting some certain truth. Such objections have been made, and they are valid against some exaggerated forms of the doctrine, but not against its substantial import. Schleiermacher alleged that the current conception of Satan is composed of several incompatible ideas, those of the divine agent for detecting evil, of the Zoroastrian evil principle, and of the angel of death ; also that persistent wickedness is not consistent with profound insight, and that an organised kingdom of evil is not possible, since evil is essentially dividing and disorganising. Now, certainly, any view that regards Satan as an essentially evil being, or invests him with the divine attributes of ubiquity or omniscience, is impossible, and inconsistent with pure Theism. It is only in a qualified sense that we can speak of Satan as embodying an evil principle ; and if we regard him, not as absolutely and essentially evil, but simply as a being created good, but fallen and depraved, his existence and character involve nothing more mysterious than that of many human monsters of cruelty and wickedness, many of whom have also had high intellectual powers. That he is sometimes represented as employed by God to detect or chastise the sins of men, is not substantially different from what is said of Sennacherib and Nebuchadnezzar. In what sense Satan is the prince of a kingdom of evil, and in what ways he tempts and assails men, is not clearly explained in Scripture; but though we may not be able to explain these things completely, there is nothing in them that can be shown to be impossible. The general conclusion of modern theologians, even of the school of Schleiermacher, such as Nitzsch, Martensen, and Dorner, seems a cautious and sound one, that the conception of Satan is one which, with our present knowledge, we cannot logically complete, and which the teaching of Scripture does not enable us to complete, but that there is nothing contradictory to reason or to facts in what is revealed on the subject.

The existence and agency of Satan, though taught in the Bible, is not properly a theological doctrine. It is nowhere used in Scripture to solve the problem of evil, or to afford a ground or principle for any part of God's dealings with men. The use that Christ and His disciples make of it is a practical one, chiefly to inculcate the need of vigilance, earnestness, and prayer in striving against evil. Against an unseen spiritual foe we need help from above; and we require not merely to watch our particular actions, but to acquire habits of Christian virtue, that will make us proof against subtle unconscious influences, as well as sudden temptation. This is that panoply of God, the necessity of which Paul enforces by a vivid description of our spiritual adversaries (Eph. vi. 10-18). At the same time, the work of Christ, by which we are saved from sin, is represented as the more glorious and wonderful, because it is a conquest of sin, not in man only, but in the whole universe.

In regard to the Fall of man, the fact that it was occasioned by the temptation of the serpent obviously affords no solution of the difficulty as to the origin of evil, nor is it presented in Scripture as doing so. Whatever partial explanation it may be held to give only removes the mystery a step farther back, since in any case there must have been a first sin to which there was no tempter. Even in the case of man, too, the temptation of the serpent was not really the cause of his sin, and does not excuse his guilt. Our first parents were created upright, but mutable; they were permitted by God's wise and holy providence to act for themselves in the exercise of their own free will; the possibility of sin and its apparent advantages were brought before them by a wicked creature in the form of temptation; but none of these things explain more than the possibility of their sin, the fact of it was due entirely to themselves, as they were brought to confess when dealt with by God for it.

But such an act of disobedience could not have been done without having an effect for evil on the character of the agents themselves. It would at once and entirely destroy their innocence, and interrupt their communion with God; and the narrative in Genesis depicts, in a simple and child-like form, but in a way most true to human nature, how their sin led to guilty shame and fear, shrinking from God's presence, insincere and ungenerous attempts to excuse themselves and throw the blame on others, or even on God Himself. The tendency of one sin is ever to lead on to others, and by degrees to form a habit of sinning that may strengthen till it grows into a second nature. This has been very clearly and convincingly shown by Bishop Butler,[1] where he explains how upright creatures may fall, and says: "It is impossible to say how much even the first full overt act of irregularity might disorder the inward constitution, unsettle the adjustments and alter the proportions which formed it, and in which the uprightness of its make consisted; but repetition of irregularities would produce habits. And thus the constitution

[1] *Analogy*, Part I. ch. v.

would be spoiled, and creatures made upright become corrupt and depraved in their settled character, proportionably to their repeated irregularities in occasional acts." Along with this, however, ought to be considered Dr. Chalmers' remarks on it,[1] in which he criticises it as making the Fall more gradual than Scripture represents it to have been, and supplements Butler's statements by emphasising the peculiar effect of a first transgression in its religious aspect, as at once destroying the harmony between God and man. In the language of Scripture, man being alienated from the favour and fellowship of God, passed at once into that state which is described as death in sin.

[1] Prelections on Butler's *Analogy*, etc.

CHAPTER IX.

THE BIBLICAL DOCTRINE OF NATIVE DEPRAVITY.

SINCE the universality of sin among men is explained in the Bible by the doctrine that human nature is in a state of disorder, which is more consistent with the facts of the case than any other explanation, theologians have endeavoured to draw from Scripture and experience a more precise conception of the character, extent, and origin of that disorder. These inquiries now claim our attention in their order.

The character that Christian thinkers have generally assigned to the moral disorder of human nature is indicated by the names they have given to it—Native Depravity, Corruption of Nature, and Original Sin. These terms all describe the same things; for though the last of them, "original sin," has been sometimes used in a wider sense, as including two things, viz. (1) original sin imputed, *i.e.* the guilt of Adam's first sin; and (2) original sin inherent, *i.e.* the corruption of man's nature,—it has been more generally restricted to the latter; and this usage is much to be preferred, since it conduces to clearness to avoid classing together two so different things under one name.[1]

In these terms it is to be observed, first, that the evil denoted by them is described as something abnormal; it is depravity,

[1] It is in the narrower and more correct sense that the term is used in the Westminster Standards; for though in the Shorter Catechism (18) the clause, "which is commonly called original sin," might be construed as referring to the whole of what precedes, the singular "is" makes it more natural to refer it to the last mentioned only; and the Confession of Faith (ch. vi. § 4, 5, 6) clearly defines original sin as "corruption of nature." So also does the Church of England, Art. IX.

corruption, sin. This is warranted by the way in which Christ and His apostles speak of men in their unrenewed state as corrupt, comparing them to rotten trees (Matt. vii. 17, 18), and describing the old man which Christians put off as being corrupted (Eph. iv. 22, etc.).

The same thing appears from the facts of the case. There is no natural tendency in man that is in itself evil, but evil arises from their disorderly working. The various appetites, desires, and affections are in themselves good, and necessary for the existence and welfare of the race; but when they act in improper directions, or with excessive force, they lead instead to destruction and misery. But there is no immoral act or habit that cannot be traced back to some impulse or principle that might have been so guided as to lead to good and useful acts, and that could not have been wanting in our nature without serious loss. Of all sins of sensual indulgence it is plain that, without the appetites from the abuse of which they spring, the human race could not exist and be propagated; sins of anger, revenge, violence, are perversions of the righteous indignation against wrong, which is a mainstay of human society; sins of selfishness, ambition, avarice, are misdirected and excessive applications of that prudent self-regard, without which the balance of human nature would be lost; and so it is in regard to all other sins. Now, if this be so, we must clearly consider the evil in man as something contrary to his true nature, a corruption of his constitution. Just as we can tell the difference between a machine that has been rudely and imperfectly made, and one that has been marred and disordered; so we can see by examining the moral nature and character of man, that his prevailing tendency to evil is not due to an imperfection, but to a corruption of his nature. This has seldom been more clearly or beautifully brought out than by Pascal in his *Pensées*, where he dwells on the greatness and misery of man as indicating a corrupt state, and thus shows, against the theory most current in the Church of Rome, that the sinful state of man implies something more than the loss of a supernatural gift, such as original righteousness is conceived by most Roman Catholics to be. If we would be true to conscience and Scripture, we must recognise a corruption of a nature essentially good, and hence we speak, not of pravity, but of depravity. The recognition of this is an element of hope in our sinful state. As Westcott well puts it, "Such an idea is, I will venture to say, a necessary condition of human hope. No view of life can be so inexpressibly sad as that which denies the Fall. If evil belongs to man as man, there appears to be no prospect of relief, here or hereafter" (*The Historic Faith*, pp. 66, 67).

But this disorder of our moral state is further described by theologians as native depravity, original or birth sin.[1] By this is meant that it is not acquired at any later period of life, but exists in every man from his birth. Some particular bad habits are contracted by acts of sin in the course of a man's life, so that it may be detected when and how he became avaricious, or ambitious, or a slave to any other vice. But there is no trace in any man's life of a time when he was free from all moral evil, or of any act to which a first beginning of his sin can be attributed. The men who have had the deepest sense of sin, and the most earnest desire to escape from it, have been the readiest to express their conviction that it has its roots in their being from the very beginning of their life as the Psalmist cries, "Behold, I was shapen in iniquity; and in sin did my mother conceive me" (Ps. li. 5), and Paul says, "We all were by nature children of wrath, even as others" (Eph. ii. 3).

This depravity is called by Paul "the sin that dwelleth in me" (Rom. vii. 17), and "the law of sin in my members" (*ib.* 23, 25), and described as a power opposing and obstructing his desires and efforts to obey the law of God. Now, a power of this kind

---

[1] The term "natural" is sometimes used in this sense; but since in a true and important sense sin is unnatural, or against nature, and since, in connection with man's inability to save himself, natural is used with a different meaning, it is better to avoid applying it to depravity at all, and to employ instead the unambiguous "native" or "connate."

can only consist of passions or desires which the will cannot control or resist, and so Paul describes it in Rom. vii. 5 ; Eph. ii. 3 ; or else in habits which have been originally formed by the indulgence of such desires. Both would seem to be included, and, indeed, they cannot be separated ; for habits are just desires or impulses become fixed, and working automatically. Such desires are also described as leading to sin by James (i. 14, 15, iv. 1, 2), Peter (1 Pet. ii. 11, iv. 2, 3 ; 2 Pet. i. 4), and John (1 John ii. 15-17).

But such desires are sinful only because they are excessive and unrestrained, and they are so when the power that should restrain them is absent or in abeyance. What is that power? Prudence, conscience—these have some effect, but only so far as they are felt to be the voice of God ; it is the fear and love of God alone that can completely moderate and rightly guide human passions. If God, as the holy and righteous governor, still more as the loving Father of men, were present to the mind, and regarded with due reverence and love by the heart, those excesses of desires and passions that violate His law and grieve His heart would not be indulged ; and were God's love and fellowship enjoyed as the true and satisfying portion of the soul, those insatiable desires that run destructive riot because they can find no adequate object in all earthly things, would be at rest and peace. This may be illustrated by the way in which Paul, bidding the Colossians (iii. 5) mortify their members on the earth, traces the prevalent sin of fornication to its root. Its immediate antecedent is "uncleanness," impure conduct of a less extreme form ; behind that is "passion"; behind that again "evil desire"; and then "covetousness," the desire of more, in the way of enjoyment as well as of possession, and of that he says emphatically, "which is idolatry," the setting up of another and earthly object of worship besides the true God, who would really satisfy the endless cravings of the soul. When God is absent, some idol must come into the place—if not sensual pleasure, as in this case, then knowledge, power, fame, wealth, or what not ; and any of them will lead, by a similar course, to sins of various kinds. Thus the radical disorder of man's moral state is ungodliness; and the Reformers well defined original sin when they said that it consisted of want of fear and trust in God, and evil desire flowing from that.

The extent of this corruption of our nature is next to be considered, more particularly with reference to the practical question whether we can by any means free ourselves from it. The statements of Scripture have led the most of those who take it for their guide to believe that the degree of corruption is such that we cannot free ourselves from it, but must be delivered by the power of God graciously exerted by His Holy Spirit working in our hearts. This belief has been generally expressed by the statement that the native depravity of man is total, and that he is unable of himself to turn from sin to God, or to prepare himself for so doing. These statements, however, require to be explained before we can rightly appreciate the grounds of them; and we must consider the two points separately.

When it is said that man's native depravity is total, it is not meant that there is nothing in any sense good in him. This would be to assert what is not true; for there are undeniably in ungodly men affections and actions that are, so far as they go, kind, upright, and beneficent. Jesus says, for example, that men, though they are evil, know how to give good gifts to their children; and the Lord says by Malachi, "A son honoureth his father, and a servant his master: if then I be a father, where is my honour? and if I be a master, where is my fear?" The good affections and acts of men towards their fellow-men but show more glaringly their undutifulness to God.

That the doctrine of total depravity as taught by the Protestant Churches does not exclude or deny such natural goodness or, as it was frequently called, "civil righteousness" (*justitia civilis*), appears plainly from the statements of their Confessions of Faith. The Augsburg Confession, the most generally received of them all, and especially representing the Lutheran Church, says:

"Art. 18. Concerning free will, they teach that man's will hath some power to perform a civil justice, and to make choice of things that are within the reach of reason." The Synod of Dort, representing all the Reformed Churches, says: "There are still in lapsed man some remains of the light of nature; by virtue whereof he retaineth some principles concerning God and things natural, and of the difference between good and evil; as also he showeth some care of virtue, and of outward discipline" (chs. iii. and iv. art. 4). And the Westminster Confession, which in ch. vi. makes an extreme and unqualified statement of the corruption of man's whole nature, elsewhere declares that even in his fallen state he has a natural knowledge of God and duty (ch. i. § 1, and xxi. § 1), "that his will is endowed with that natural liberty, that it is neither forced nor by any absolute necessity of nature determined to good or evil" (ch. ix. § 1); and that "works done by unregenerate men for the matter of them may be things which God commands, and of good use both to themselves and others" (ch. xvi. § 7). The same thing is recognised by the best Calvinistic theologians, such as Dr. Chalmers and Dr. Hodge.[1]

It follows from this, and it is also the plain teaching of Scripture, that there are many different degrees of sin and guilt among unregenerated men. Some are not far from the kingdom of God, while others may be on the verge of that blasphemy against the Holy Spirit for which there is no forgiveness. Evil men wax worse and worse; some sin in ignorance, others are described as hardening themselves, and giving themselves over to work all uncleanness with greediness.

But depravity may be called total, in the sense of affecting all the parts of our being, producing an entire alienation from God, and leaving in us no recuperative power or tendency, if left to ourselves, to return to God. This is what theologians mean to

[1] A very striking representation of it is given by the Puritan John Howe in his beautiful description of fallen man as the deserted and ruined temple of God (*The Living Temple*, Part II. ch. 4).

assert when they speak of total depravity; it is the corruption of our whole nature; and this we think is borne out both by experience and by Scripture.

The phenomena that lead us to recognise depravity in general, point also to its not being limited to any one part of our nature. Abnormal and evil tendencies appear in them all; we observe not only violence and excess in the appetites and passions, but blindness or perversity in the intellect, dulness or obliquity in the conscience, weakness or obstinacy in the will. In fact, it is hard to conceive of any moral injury to human nature in one part that would not somehow affect the whole. The more complex that nature may be supposed to be, the more probable does it become that any defect or excess in one part of it would injure the whole. The moral uprightness of man consists in this, that all the various propensities of his nature are kept in due balance and control. If any one of them is habitually excessive, those that should balance it must be in the same degree weakened, and the reason and conscience, which should discern truth and right, must be blinded, and the will, which should enforce the dictates of reason and conscience, weakened and perverted.

Scripture describes all the parts of human nature as affected by moral depravity in regard to God and the things of God; and a consideration of some of the passages in which different faculties are spoken of may throw light on the subject.

In regard to the intellect, the fullest statement is by Paul (1 Cor. i. 18–ii. 16), where he declares that the word of the cross is foolishness to the wise of this world; that the world by wisdom knew not God, nor the things that are revealed by the Spirit of God. The natural man ($\psi\nu\chi\iota\kappa\delta\varsigma$, under the guidance of the soul as distinct from the spirit) receiveth not the things of the Spirit of God, neither can he know them, because they are spiritually discerned. This clearly implies that worldly men cannot discern divine truth, either because what Paul here calls spirit is absent, or because it is so weakened and overpowered by the soul that the entire man may be called animal and not spiritual. The latter is certainly Paul's meaning, for he nowhere speaks of the unregenerate as destitute of any part or faculty of human nature, but positively speaks of them as possessing mind (νοῦς, Tit. i. 15), which he seems here (1 Cor. ii. 18) to identify with spirit. If, now, we inquire further how we are to conceive of the intellect as disabled in reference to divine things, we may refer to our Lord's words to Peter, when he was offended at the cross in the same way as those of whom Paul is speaking, "Thou mindest not the things of God, but the things of men" (Matt. xvi. 23); thou art under the influence of sense (ψυχή), not of a divinely-enlightened mind that knows what is worthy of the Son of God. Compare also John's words, "He that loveth not, knoweth not God; for God is love" (1 John iv. 8); and James' description of the earthly and the heavenly wisdom (Jas. iii. 13-18).

From this it appears that the mind of man is darkened in regard to God and divine things by the absence of that pure and holy love through which God is known, and the prevalence of those notions that come through the senses and are worldly or selfish.

Another passage in Paul's writings, where the effects of sin on different parts of man's being are described, is Eph. iv. 17-19. "That ye no longer walk as the Gentiles also walk, in the vanity of their mind" (τοῦ νοός). The mind here is the higher part of our intellectual nature, the reason or power of intuition by which we apprehend first principles or necessary truths of faith and duty: to this is ascribed vanity, *i.e.* emptiness, unprofitableness, so that it does not apprehend what is real and truly good. Then he proceeds, "being darkened in their understanding," *i.e.* the reasoning faculty, "alienated from the life of God because of the ignorance that is in them, because of the hardness of their hearts." The last two clauses are clearly parallel, and it makes practically no difference whether both together are the reasons of the two preceding ones, or more specifically the ignorance is the cause of the darkness of the understanding and the hardness is the cause of the alienation from the life of God, *i.e.* the life which God lives

G

in Himself and communicates to those who are born of the spirit, the life of love. Further, Paul goes on to describe the practical result of this state of darkness and callousness, "who, being past feeling, have given themselves over to wantonness, to work all uncleanness with greediness." This is no doubt a description of an extreme degree of depravity, and of the gross forms of evil in which it showed itself. But we see from it how all the various parts of human nature in its corrupt state act and react on each other; and Paul goes on to describe as the only remedy for it, not merely an enlightened mind, or a sensitive conscience, or a tender heart, but what includes all these, "a new man created after God in righteousness and holiness of truth" (ver. 24); truth enlightening the understanding and satisfying the mind; holiness or piety awakening the affections and elevating them to God, and righteousness showing itself in that love which is the fulfilling of the law.

CHAPTER X.

INABILITY OF MAN TO DELIVER HIMSELF.

THE chief practical stress of the question as to total depravity turns on the second point before noted as involved in it, the absence of any recuperative tendency or power; for it is at this point that the question raised by this doctrine touches upon another, that of the possibility or impossibility of men raising themselves, or doing anything to raise themselves, from this state of moral depravity. If this be possible, it would seem that it is so, because some part or faculty of our nature is only partially or not at all affected by moral depravity, and so that is not total but only partial. Such, in fact, has generally been the view of those who have held that man can do something to recover himself. The Greek Fathers of the Alexandrian and Antiochian schools, Clemens Alex., Origen, Athanasius, Chrysostom, etc.,[1] held that the corruption of human nature resided in the body and the animal soul ($\psi v \chi \acute{\eta}$), but that the spirit ($\pi v \varepsilon \tilde{v} \mu \alpha$), in which they included reason, conscience, and will, was not corrupted; the two former of these above named going so far as to say that it is not at all affected; the two latter, and the later Greek Fathers generally, holding that it is affected, but only indirectly. Their doctrine was very nearly what was called in the West Semi-Pelagianism. In modern times it is chiefly the will that has been held to be exempt from depravity.

There is some plausibility in this view, because the will of man has a certain freedom that is inalienable from it, and without which there would be no responsibility. If the mere faculty of

[1] See Shedd, *History of Christian Doctrine*, vol. ii.

volition be viewed by itself, apart from all the other faculties of the soul, it may be said to remain intact. Philosophers are divided in opinion as to what the essential freedom of the will is, some holding it to imply a power of determining either to act or not, or to act in one way or another, in presence of various desires, affections, and judgments moving to action; while others hold it to imply only the absence of constraint, and the exercise of rational liking, but to be quite consistent with the will being invariably determined by the desires, affections, and judgments.

It is admitted on both sides that the will can control all the external actions, but that it has no power to originate desires, affections, or judgments; but those who maintain the liberty of self-determination hold that it can and should decide whether to act upon them or not, and in the case of desires and affections, that it is able either to check or to indulge them. This it can do by means of the power of directing the attention to one object or another. In this way also men can by degrees either strengthen or weaken the power of desires, affections, and judgments of the mind over their conduct, and so, to a considerable extent, mould and modify their character. If we accept this view of free will, as I think we should, then we shall acknowledge that the will of man, even now in the state of sin, has power to modify the character, and strengthen or weaken the effect of desires, affections, and judgments, by means of the direction of the attention.

This power, however, admits of degrees, and requires exercise in order to be maintained and strengthened. If a man does not exert the power of attention, but allows his action to be swayed by desire, emotion, or affection, he will find it increasingly difficult to check such impulses by reflection; whereas, if he directs his mind habitually to objects of thought that are opposed to them, he will gain self-command, and have ever more and more control over his passions.

When this power of the will diminishes by disuse so as to

become practically ineffective, the will may properly be said to be enslaved (*servum arbitrium*), as it is frequently described in Scripture (John viii. 34; Rom. vi. 16, 17; Titus iii. 3; 2 Pet. ii. 19).

The mere diminution of the power of the will implies of necessity a preponderance of evil, because the judgments of the intellect do not directly impel to action, as the desires and affections do; though the will may be guided by them, it needs an interposition of volition that they may lead to action. Hence when the will is simply inactive, the conduct is determined merely by whatever desire or affection may be strongest, and the dictates of reason and conscience are disregarded. Still more if the will positively decides for what is evil, it may by turning the attention to objects of temptation give a more positive evil bias to the character, which may become strengthened by habit into a second nature. But in such a case the power of the will is not really strengthening, though it may seem to be so. For by deliberately exciting the passions, as well as indulging them, a man is allowing them to gain more strength, and so making it more difficult to control them, even when from motives of prudence or a sense of duty he may wish to do so. Thus confirmed habits of sin are properly called bondage or slavery, while those of virtue are not so. A man is the slave of his vices, but not of his virtues; because in doing good he exercises a rational choice, and controls his passions and the allurements of temptation.

It is quite clear that the power of the will to control by its volitions all the outward actions, does not imply an ability to do what is in any true sense spiritually good or acceptable to God. For nothing is more emphatically taught in Scripture than this, that God looks not merely on the outward conduct, but on the heart, and is not pleased with any obedience in deeds that does not proceed from love in the heart. Granted, therefore, that men can reform their external conduct by the exercise of their own will, that does not prove that they can convert themselves; the question is, Can they change their hearts? and if this is possible at all, it can only be, not by a direct exercise of will, but only by that indirect power, which the will has, to control and modify the affections and desires by the direction of the attention to objects fitted to check or direct them aright. In point of fact, however, we believe that, even in this way, men in their fallen state are not able so to mould their character as to produce real repentance, faith, and love to God.

The inability that Augustinian theologians ascribe to the will of man to any spiritual good, does not necessarily imply that the general power of the will to control by attention the desires and affections, is less than it would have been had man not fallen. That may be so, but we have no conclusive evidence of it, since the facts may be explained without that assumption. The fact to be explained is, that men by nature are so averse to God, that they cannot, without the gracious influence of His Spirit, make themselves godly. This is the testimony of Scripture (John iii. 3, 5, v. 44, vi. 44, 65, xii. 39; Rom. viii. 7, 8; Eph. ii. 1-3, iv. 17, 19; Matt. xii. 34; 2 Pet. ii. 10-14, 18-20); it has been the conviction of many of the holiest and wisest of men, and it seems to be borne out by experience. A certain amount of reformation of character may be effected by men's own will, with no more aid than teaching. If, for instance, a selfish and self-indulgent man be thoroughly convinced that it is right and proper to deny himself for the sake of his family, or to devote himself to the service of his country, he may by degrees so act that the selfish desires shall be checked, and the family or patriotic affections come to rule his conduct; and thus he may, in course of time, change his character from a selfish to a benevolent one. The will can do this, because the natural affections towards his family and country are in the soul, though they had been overborne by the selfish desires and habits. If they had been entirely lost, the will could not have produced them; it can only decide between motives to action, not create any new one. So, if love to God and to goodness were as natural to man as family affections are, even in very depraved men, it would be possible for the will, by the indirect exercise of its power of directing the attention, to acquire by degrees a truly godly character. But this would seem not to be possible for man left to himself. At least, those who have been most undoubtedly godly, have always ascribed their piety, not to their own efforts, but to the gracious influence of God's Spirit. On the other hand, those who have thought that men can reform themselves by their own will, if only they are rightly taught, have either limited that reformation to man's duties to his fellows, confessing that they know not how to serve God, as Confucius and the Chinese sages did; or when they have, like the Jewish Pharisees and rationalists among Christians, sought to produce piety by teaching, it has been of an outward and formal, or of a low and cold kind. A love to God for His own sake cannot be created by mere adventitious considerations; it is, according to the teaching of Scripture, awakened by God's love to us, shed abroad in our hearts by the Holy Spirit given to us.

There is therefore good ground for maintaining the doctrine of man's inability by nature to anything spiritually good and well-pleasing to God. This just means that he cannot of himself change his heart, or turn the bias of his inclinations from sin to God.

To this doctrine, however, there has always been made an objection, which is very natural and plausible, and deserves to be met and answered. It is, that it is inconsistent with responsibility, inasmuch as a man cannot be justly blamed, or held accountable, for not doing what he has no power to do. Now, it must be admitted that it would be a fatal objection to the doctrine, if it really were incompatible with man's responsibility. For moral guilt is inseparably connected with sin, and it is uniformly assumed and taught in Scripture, that the depravity of sinners is not merely their misfortune, but their fault; and that they are accountable and blameworthy, both for it and for all that they do under its influence. We must therefore accept the principle, or major premiss of the objection, which is, that no doctrine that subverts man's responsibility can be true; and the only way in which we can answer it is, by showing that the doctrine of the sinner's inability to convert himself and serve God aright does not subvert his responsibility.

Now, there is a kind of inability that is inconsistent with responsibility, that which arises from the want of faculties for doing anything, or from a restraint put upon us from without. A blind man is not responsible for not reading the word of God, nor an ignorant, unintellectual peasant for not understanding all the deep things contained in it. Paul, when in prison, was not to blame for not going about to preach the gospel. These are things for which, in the cases supposed, the power or the liberty is denied, and the obligation in duty ceases along with them. For in all such cases there may be a most sincere willingness, nay, an eager desire, to do the things in question; and as God looks, not to the outward act, but to the heart, and regards the state of that as the chief, and indeed only valuable thing, He does not hold men guilty for not doing what they are really anxious to do, but are prevented, against their own will, from actually doing. " If there be first a willing mind, it is accepted according to that a man hath, not according to that he hath not." If the inability of sinners were of this kind, it would indeed subvert their responsibility.

But there is another kind of inability of which this cannot be said, one that arises, not from want of faculties nor from external constraint, but from the state of the heart; when a person, for example, is so selfish, or so avaricious, or so ambitious, that no amount of persuasion would induce him to do a generous or self-sacrificing act, we say, he cannot exercise self-denial, he is incapable of disinterested goodness; but we do not for a moment imagine that this excuses him, it rather makes him guiltier, and deserving of greater blame. This inability has its seat in the heart; and since it is the heart that gives value to moral conduct, the wickedness of heart that absolutely prevents a good action is itself the greatest degree of vice.

This has generally been called "moral inability," as distinguished from "natural inability," which is that which results from constraint or want of faculties; and in this sense it is right to say, that man's inability to do what is spiritually good is not natural, but moral; though in another sense of the term it is properly called natural by Dr. Hodge, as belonging to us from birth, and not acquired by habit. It seems better, however, in order to avoid confusion, to express this by calling it "native or innate," reserving the term "natural" for the other meaning.

Now the inability of the sinner to turn to God is of the latter kind; it does not arise from the limitation of our faculties, or from external restraint, but from the ungodliness of the heart It is because the mind of the flesh is enmity against God that it is not subject to the law of God, neither indeed can be (Rom. viii. 7). This is not an inability that is consistent with an earnest desire to do the thing required; on the contrary, it arises from an intense aversion to it. It is not therefore inconsistent with responsibility; it does not lessen the blame due to sin, for it just indicates the great depth and strength of man's depravity.

It is to be observed, however, that what we ascribe to sinners in regard to spiritual good, is a real inability, and not a mere unwillingness or disinclination, though it has its seat in the heart, and may be regarded as an extreme degree of disinclination. It is one thing for a man to be merely unwilling to perform an act of self-denial, though he might easily be induced to do it; and quite a different thing to have such a habit of selfish indulgence, that no persuasion would move him to self-denial. The latter, and not merely the former, is the state of man, as described in Scripture, in relation to holiness and repentance towards God. It seems, therefore, necessary to speak of inability as well as of unwillingness, and our Lord and the sacred writers use both expressions, "ye will not," "ye cannot" (John v. 39, 44). It is not true or right to say to men, as some do, that they can repent and obey God's law if they will; at least that is an ambiguous and misleading expression. In a sense it may be true; for if only men were willing, there is no other obstacle in the way of their turning to God. But it is apt to be understood as meaning that by a mere act of volition they can turn their hearts to God; and this is a dangerous error. If men are led to think that they can do so, they will be led to rely on their own efforts and resolutions, and omit to pray for help from God; and also may be tempted to delay repentance, under the idea that they can repent and save themselves at any time they please; whereas, if they are shown that the inclination of their hearts to evil is such that they cannot by their own power overcome or change it, they will be more ready at once and without delay to ask in prayer the aid of God's grace.

It is also to be remembered, that though men cannot convert themselves, there is nothing in this doctrine to prevent them, but everything to induce them, to pray to God to convert them, to take away their evil and hard heart, and give them a good and tender one; nay, this is the very thing that the doctrine should lead them to do. God is ever ready to answer such prayers. He has promised to give the Holy Spirit to them that ask Him. He exercises indeed a sovereignty in this matter, but it is a sovereignty of grace. He often sends His Holy Spirit to awaken and convert those who are not asking or seeking for it; but He never refuses the gift of that blessed agent to any who ask it. This should be borne in mind in considering man's responsibility for not turning to God, though he is under a moral inability of doing so; that not only does this inability consist of extreme disinclination, but it would be overcome and removed by the Spirit of God, if the sinner only prayed to God for that. He must, indeed, pray to God with a humble confession that he has no right to His help; he must confess the sin and guilt of his evil life and evil heart, and cast himself entirely on the mercy of God, which is sovereign and free; he should acknowledge that his prayer is no more free from defect and sin than his heart, but we know that God is the hearer of prayer, to whom all flesh may come; and while we have to confess that iniquities prevail against us, we are encouraged to add in faith, "as for our transgressions, Thou shalt purge them away" (Ps. lxv. 2, 3).

The difference of natural and moral inability has also been expressed in modern times by the distinction of formal and real freedom. The inability of the natural man to spiritual good has frequently been described by theologians as the bondage of the will to sin (*servitus voluntatis, servum arbitrium*), or the want of freedom to good. This phraseology has, indeed, often led to confusion and misunderstanding, but it is founded on Scripture; for our Lord says, "Every one that committeth sin is the bondservant of sin" (John viii. 34); and Paul uses similar language in Rom. vi. 16-22. So also 2 Pet. ii. 19. According to this view, Christ alone gives true freedom, and they only have it who trust in Him and follow Him. This freedom consists in deliverance from the power of corruption, which is contrary to our true nature and destiny, as made by God for Himself, and in being enabled to obey God's law from the heart, not out of constraint or fear, but as the law of our mind, in which we delight. This is what is called "real freedom"; and it is so far from excluding certainty, or implying the possibility of acting otherwise, that in its highest degree it implies the certainty of right actions, and the impossibility of any others (*non posse peccare*). Such is the freedom of God Himself, who is essentially holy, so that He cannot lie, He cannot deny Himself.

This state is truly called freedom; because the good, even though invariably chosen, is willingly chosen, by no constraint from without; and because it is in accordance with the nature of God, and the truest nature of man, as made in the image of God. When a man is under the power of sin, even though he may be so willingly, he does not possess real freedom; because sin is contrary to his true nature, and there is always something in him that protests against it, however weakly and ineffectually.

But there is a sense in which man must be regarded as free, even when he has not that real freedom which Christ alone can give. This is not only a dictate of reason and consciousness, but is recognised in Scripture as well, since men are described as doing what they listed (Matt. xvii. 12), as they will (Mark xiv. 7), having power as touching his own will (1 Cor. vii. 57), etc. Modern writers call this "formal freedom"; the Westminster divines describe it under the name of "natural liberty" (Conf. ix. 1). By whatever name it is known, it forms the indispensable basis of responsibility. But there have been great disputes among philosophers as to what it is and how it is related to real freedom.

Some hold that formal freedom always implies the power of contrary choice, so that in every case where one acts or wills freely, it must be possible that he should have acted or willed otherwise. Those who hold this generally mean, not only that subjectively the agent has the power to will a certain thing or not, but also that objectively it must be possible he should do either, so that there can be no certainty of the issue. Hence liberty so conceived has often been called liberty of indifference or of contingency.[1] If this view be adopted, then formal freedom is made to be absolutely inconsistent, not only with any bondage of the will to sin, but even with perfect real freedom, as before described, for that implies a certainty of choosing good. Accordingly, with this conception of formal freedom there are only two alternatives.

One is to deny real freedom entirely, and to hold that as the possibility of a contrary choice is essential to freedom and responsibility, man never can be in a state in which good is impossible for him, and equally not in one in which evil is impossible. This was the view of the Pelagians in the ancient Church, of Duns Scotus and others of the schoolmen, of the Jesuits in the Church of Rome, and of Socinians and Arminians among

[1] In every volition, it may be said with truth, that we are conscious of, and therefore have, the power of willing otherwise. But we are also conscious that there are some things that we certainly shall not will; and therefore our consciousness of the power of contrary choice is not inconsistent with the certainty of our choosing in one way and not another, and does not imply the objective possibility, all things considered, of either choice.

Protestants. It is, however, opposed to the facts of man's moral state by nature, as well as to the representations of Scripture.

The other alternative is that adopted by Julius Müller. He holds that formal freedom is, indeed, inconsistent with real freedom, but that it was only a preliminary stage to it. The possibility of a contrary choice is, indeed, implied in formal freedom, but this is lost when man becomes a slave to sin; and when he is restored from that state, and brought to have real freedom in such a degree that he cannot sin (1 John iii. 9), formal freedom is excluded. But what of man's responsibility, for is not formal freedom necessary for that? Müller admits and maintains that it is necessary to trace the origin of sin to a free act, in order to exclude it from the divine causality; but with his definition of formal freedom he can find in the empirical life of man no such freedom, hence he is obliged to trace back the original fall of each man to a pre-existent state.[1] That is a hypothesis destitute of all positive evidence either from nature or revelation, and accordingly it has been adopted by very few.

Thus on either alternative this conception of formal freedom seems to lead to untenable conclusions. Philosophically also it is an extreme position, very difficult to reconcile with facts, and not accepted by many who are far from holding the opinion that the will is invariably determined by motives.[2]

But there is another view of the freedom that is essential to responsibility, taken by Augustine and most Augustinian theologians, who have so defined it that it is not inconsistent with real freedom, but may coexist either with it or with the absence of it. It is conceived as being spontaneity or rational liking (*lubentia rationalis*). This implies the absence of force or coercion from without, and some have spoken as if this were all that is necessary for responsibility. But the wisest defenders of this view hold another element to be implied in formal freedom, the absence

---

[1] See his *Christian Doctrine of Sin*, Book III. Division 1, where the whole subject is very fully and ably discussed.
[2] See Calderwood's *Handbook of Moral Philosophy*, Part III.

of any natural necessity from within, or, in the language of Kant, that the volition may be determined, not merely by laws, but by the presentation of laws to the intellect. That a man is not constrained from without, does not prove him to be free; that may be said of a tree growing, or of an animal following its instincts. It is also true of man, that in his moral acts he is not determined by any such natural necessity. Whatever influences act upon him to hinder him from doing good or evil, are not either outward constraint or physical impulse, but such as act through his intellectual and moral nature by conceptions, emotions, affections, and the like. These two elements of natural liberty are indicated in the Westminster Confession (ix. 1), that the will of man is "neither forced, nor by any absolute necessity of nature determined, to good or evil." This freedom belongs essentially to the will in all the different states, of innocence, of sin, of grace, and of glory, which are described in the following sections of the chapter.

It is of vital importance for the understanding of Augustinian and Calvinistic theology to remember that its advocates maintain the possibility of men being certainly determined either to good or evil without being either forced, or necessitated by any physical law. This is constantly forgotten by opponents; and so the doctrines of the bondage of the will, of efficacious grace, and certain perseverance, are supposed to imply compulsion, and to exclude freedom of any kind. Hence it is that so many representations of Calvinism are mere caricatures. If our distinctions are unreal, let that be proved; but unless they are understood and attended to, no correct understanding of our doctrine is possible.

CHAPTER XI.

THE INHERITANCE AND IMPUTATION OF SIN.

THE distinction between natural and moral inability, and between formal and real freedom, serves to a certain degree to meet the difficulty raised by the fact that man is unable to deliver himself from the bondage of sin, while yet he feels himself to blame, and is blamed and judged by God for his sin. It removes the difficulty so far as it is a moral one, affecting the dictates of our own conscience; for it shows that we are not in bondage against our will, and are under no constraint or natural incapacity hindering us from doing what is right. No one who clearly understands, that by moral inability or bondage is meant simply an overmastering love of what is sinful, can really think that this is an excuse for doing what we know to be wrong; and the general judgment of mankind, that bad temper, or ill-nature, or wrong habits, do not remove responsibility, confirms that conclusion. So far as our own conscience is concerned, the objection is completely silenced.

But this consideration does not remove the difficulty which presents itself from a wider, more objective, and theological view of the facts. We are conscious of a moral disease, which is antecedent to and independent of any deliberate choice of our own will, with which, therefore, we must have come into being. Now is it consistent with the holiness and justice of God to suppose that this disorder is due to Him who is our Maker? Does it not seem to make Him the author of moral evil, and so infringe on His perfect holiness? Does it not also imply that He has brought us into being inadequately furnished with moral powers, and incapable of that virtue which He requires of us; and would not this be inconsistent with fair and equitable dealing towards His creatures? These questions point to the most perplexing problem in theology,—a problem of which no completely satisfactory solution has ever been given, but on which some light is thrown by the scriptural representations of the solidarity of the human race.

The explanation which the Bible suggests of the facts of human sin and depravity consists, in general, in the representation, that mankind is an organic unity, and that as such it is an apostate race, fallen and estranged from God.

The various races of men are all represented as sprung from one stock. Eve is so called because she was the mother of all living (Gen. iii. 20), and by the sons of Noah the whole earth was overspread (ix. 19). Such is the record of the early ages; and to it Jesus referred when He traced the divine law of marriage for all men to the fact that God made man at the beginning male and female (Matt. xix. 4-6; Mark x. 6-9). So Paul declared to the Athenians that God "made of one all nations of men, to dwell on all the face of the earth" (Acts xvii. 26). The unity of the human race is the notion underlying that humanity, recognition of the rights and dignity of all men, however degraded, and feeling of brotherhood to all, which is a special mark of Christianity compared with most of the ethnic religions; and this notion, as far at least as regards the specific unity of the race, is fully borne out by science and philosophy. Whatever view be taken of the origin of mankind, all men have undoubtedly the same physical, intellectual, and moral nature; and this implies that they may have been all descended from one ancestral pair.

Whether they actually were so descended or not, science and history cannot with any certainty determine. The affinities and the genealogical relations of the languages, myths, and customs of the most widely distant nations, make it highly probable that they have been; and the principle of parsimony is adverse to the assumption of a plurality of causes for what could be explained by one; but in the absence of positive proof, these presumptions are not conclusive, and they might be overcome. Nor does Scripture lay any great stress on the assertion of the actual physical descent of all men from one pair; what it chiefly insists on is, that the first man represented all mankind, and by his fall brought sin and death on all.[1]

The facts of human nature and history point to the conclusion that God has made the whole of mankind a unity, in such a way that the characters and experiences of every member of it are inseparably connected with those of his brethren and of the entire race. No man can stand aloof by and for himself alone; whether he will or no, he is influenced by the others, and in turn influences them. We do so in many different ways; but probably the most powerful, though the most mysterious, is that of heredity. The characters of parents are reproduced in their children generation after generation, and these often reap the fruit of what their fathers have sown.

Nature and history show us this as a fact, but revelation teaches us to see in it an appointment of God, who "visits the iniquity of the fathers upon the children, upon the third and upon the fourth generation of them that hate Him; and shows mercy unto a thousand generations of them that love Him, and keep His commandments" (Ex. xx. 6; Deut. vii. 9); yet so that a repentant and reforming son shall not die for the sin of his parents, nor a backsliding son be saved because of their obedience, and in the ultimate judgment the principle is "the soul that sinneth, it shall die" (Ezek. xviii.). This implies that the law of heredity is recognised by God in His dealing with mankind in the course of their history on the earth; though in the decision of the final destiny of men, individual responsibility comes to the front. All men inherit from our first parents, not only a bad example, but a nature prone to sin, and radically

---

[1] It has been said that only on the supposition of "first parents" can the universality of sin be explained; but this is not absolutely true, for Bushnell, in his *Nature and the Supernatural*, has given a view which is independent of that, and yet does not really make sin a necessity. Still the descent of all men from one pair is more probable.

disordered; and all our moral and spiritual history, and the circumstances of our conflict with temptation and sin, are affected by the first sin of the race.

In virtue of this unity of mankind, God deals with the race in its entirety as an apostate and sinful race, since the sin of its first progenitors has infected all their descendants. Hence all the calamities and sufferings, which the Bible teaches us to regard as visitations of God's holy anger against sin, come upon young children who have no knowledge of good and evil, and therefore no personal responsibility, as well as on those who are actually guilty. They suffer for the sins of their parents, and ultimately of the first man, Adam, without any actual sin of their own; and we all suffer for that first transgression, in addition to our own sins.

This fact is referred to by Paul in Rom. v. 12–21 as affording an analogy to the great truth of the gospel, that all believers are forgiven and accepted as righteous on account of the obedience and sacrifice of the one man, Jesus Christ, who is called from this very analogy "the last Adam," "the second Man" (1 Cor. xv. 45, 47; comp. 21, 22), *i.e.* the only other man who has been a representative of the whole race, and whose actions have affected all men. Because of the parallel thus plainly drawn, it has been inferred, that, as Paul says of those who are forgiven for Christ's sake, that God imputes to them righteousness apart from works (Rom. iv. 6), we may say of all men, since they suffer for the transgression of the first man, that God imputes to them sin. Hence the imputation of Adam's sin to all mankind has been generally asserted as a doctrine of theology, and has been thought by many to throw some light on the perplexing problem of the universality of sin and of suffering, although to others it has seemed rather to increase its difficulty.

It should be remembered that the term imputation, as applied to the relation of Adam's sin to mankind, is only an inference from, and not an express statement of, Scripture; and, therefore, the authority of God's word can only be pleaded for the general statement that by the offence of the one the many were made sinners, and not for the particular notions that may be conceived to be implied in imputation. Also, while Paul teaches that there is a general analogy between our ruin through Adam and our salvation through Christ, he also states that there are several very important differences between the two cases (Rom. v. 15-17); and his whole statement about the effects of the sin of the first man is incidental, and subordinate to his declarations about the salvation of Christ, which it is his main object to illustrate.

It is very important here to draw a broad and plain distinction between what the Bible really teaches on this subject and the doctrines or theories that have been drawn from it by inference and logical reasoning, frequently with the aid of the principles or results of some philosophical system or other. Such doctrines have their value as intellectual efforts to understand God's ways; but they are only theories based on Scripture, and it is wrong and dangerous to hold Scripture itself as committed to anything beyond what it really teaches. What it teaches is, that there is a unity or solidarity in the human race, in virtue of which the transgression of its first parents has entailed on all its members manifold sufferings and a tendency to sin, from which none is free. Mankind is treated by God as an apostate or sinful race, which indeed it is. The race as a whole is out of communion with God, having lost that precious blessing by the sin of its first parents. God regards men as a seed of evil-doers, and deals with them accordingly; not, indeed, in strict justice or unmixed wrath, but with mercy and with judgment. This fact, which is borne out by the moral state of the world and the course of Divine Providence, as well as by the representations of Scripture, has generally been described by theologians by the doctrine of the imputation to the whole race of the sin of its first parents. The doctrine seems a legitimate inference from the statements of Paul, that "by one man sin entered into the world, and death by sin; and so death passed unto all men, for that all sinned;" that "by the trespass of the one the many died;" that "the judgment came of one unto condemnation;" and that "by one man's disobedience the many were made sinners" (Rom. v. 12, 15, 16, 19), though it should be remembered that all these occur in one paragraph, and, therefore, they have not the force of separate and independent testimonies, and also that they are not the proper subject of Paul's teaching in this place, but incidental statements by way of illustration. However, they declare what is a great reality in regard to God's dealing with the human race, that He treats it as having a unity and solidarity, so that each man does not bear merely his own sin, but a share of that of the race; and this may be expressed by saying that the guilt of the first sin is imputed to all mankind, as well as the corruption of nature caused by it transmitted to them all. By guilt in this connection must be understood, not moral culpability (*culpa*), but legal responsibility (*reatus*), or liability to punishment.

This general statement is all that can be said to have the positive authority of Scripture; but since it goes only a little way to explain the perplexing facts of the case, theologians, for many ages past, have attempted, by means of inferential reasoning and speculation, to attain a more complete explanation, and to construct a more systematic theory about original sin and imputed guilt. Their explanations have taken different forms, and there have sometimes been keen disputes between the advocates of different theories. The differences have turned chiefly on the nature of the union or unity of the human race, in virtue of which sin and death have passed through to all men.

One theory holds that there is a real unity of substance in humanity, so that what God made at first was the whole mass of mankind, contained really or seminally in the progenitors of the race. Adam was the universal man, and all the individuals of the race are just that one generic substance that was in him, unfolded and divided out. This is the theory of Realism, dominant in the Middle Ages and held by some able men still;[1]

---

[1] As Dr. Wm. G. T. Shedd, *Dogmatic Theology* and Ernest Naville, *The Problem of Evil*.

and, according to it, God simply allowed the whole human nature to sin and become corrupt in the person of Adam, from which it necessarily followed that all his descendants were born in sin. This could not have been otherwise unless God had annihilated humanity after Adam's sin.

Another theory, without maintaining a unity of real substance in the race, and admitting that the individuals are truly distinct from Adam, yet supposes that the soul as well as the body of each one is derived by propagation from the parents. This is known as Traducianism, and has also been very largely held as an explanation of original sin.[1] According to this view, God does not immediately create the sinful soul, but brings it into being mediately, like the body; and the soul is sinful, not because God makes it so, but because it is made sinful through the souls of ancestors who have freely sinned.

A third theory is that the body only is generated by the parents, but the soul is created directly by God in each individual.[2] This is known as Creationism; and it is certainly more difficult to explain the fact of original sin on this view than on either of the former, since it regards the soul, which is the proper seat of sin, as a new creation of God in every case. Hence those who have taken this view have generally held also that there is a federal or covenant oneness of the race, in virtue of which Adam was constituted by God the representative of all his posterity, in what is called the Covenant of Works, a doctrine which has been maintained also by many who have held the other theories along with it.

Now all these different views are philosophical theories, rather than expressions of religious faith. If any of them can be established as true, this must be done by means of metaphysical or psychological reasoning. The advocates of each do indeed assert that they are founded on the revelation of Scripture, but they do not and cannot maintain that they are expressly taught

---

[1] So Luther and most of the Lutheran theologians.
[2] So Calvin and most of the theologians of the Reformed Church.

there. Each class of theologians appeals to certain statements of Scripture, and argues that the necessary inference from them is the theory he supports. Thus the Realist points to the places where it is said that Levi paid tithes in Abraham because he was in the loins of his father (Heb. vii. 9, 10); and infers that in the same way, since it is said that in Adam all die, they must have been in his loins; and again he refers to the place where Paul says that, as the potter with the clay, God makes of one lump vessels to honour and to dishonour (Rom. ix. 21, 22), and infers that human nature must be a lump (*massa corrupta*), from which individuals are formed.

The Traducianist, on his part, rests on the passage where God is said to have rested from His work of creation (Gen. ii. 2, 3), and holds that this implies that He does not create the soul of each man at his birth; also, since the soul inherits sinfulness from the parents of the race, it must itself be derived from them, else God would be the creator of a sinful soul.

The Creationist, in turn, infers his doctrine from God being called the Father of spirits (Heb. xii. 9), the God of the spirits of all flesh (Num. xvi. 22), and being said to form the spirit of man within him (Zech. xii. 1), and give spirit to them that dwell on the earth (Isa. xlii. 5).

Similarly, the doctrine that Adam was the federal representative of all his natural posterity, is based on the parallel drawn by Paul between Adam and Christ, taken together with the fact that the divine constitution by which believers receive blessings through Christ is called a covenant. Hence it is inferred that the relation of Adam to the race was also that of a covenant.

But all these are large inferences from particular statements and forms of expression in various parts of the Bible, inferences which the inspired writers cannot reasonably be supposed to have had in view when they made the statements in question; and they are inferences, not of a properly religious, but of a philosophical nature. It is, indeed, our right and duty to draw inferences from the Scriptures, and not to be content with their mere literal meaning. We may and should allow its teaching to convey to us all its natural and necessary consequences in the directions in which it really points; and we may also infer from a series of statements some general religious principle that they imply as underlying them all. What is fairly reached by such processes may properly claim the authority of the Christian revelation. But it is a very different thing to press incidental utterances to logical implications in directions entirely away from the scope of the writer, and to gather from them, not merely religious conceptions, but metaphysical systems. Who can imagine, for instance, that the writer of the Epistle to the Hebrews, in expounding the priesthood of Christ, or exhorting to patience in suffering, intended to express any opinion about the origin of human souls? To treat his words as if he did is a Rabbinical mode of exegesis, not a true grammatical and historical one.

The inference on which the federal or representative theory rests is more legitimate than these, because, although the name *covenant* is nowhere in Scripture directly given to God's dealings with our first parents, yet Paul clearly believed and taught that Adam's transgression brought sin and death on all mankind; and though, in Rom. v. and 1 Cor. xv., he introduces this as an illustration of our redemption by Christ, yet he is so careful to prove it, in Rom. v. 13, 14, that it seems to be a substantial part of his doctrine; and since it is not a philosophical but a properly religious doctrine, we may accept it on his authority. It is not proved by this that there was an express and formal covenant of God with our first parents, in a way at all similar to that in which we read of His making a covenant with Abraham or with Israel. All that is said in the Biblical narrative is that God gave Adam a command not to eat of the tree of the knowledge of good and evil, because in the day he did so he should surely die; thereby giving implicitly an assurance that so long as he obeyed he should not die. Thus we can only speak of a tacit covenant. Further, it is not said or implied that Adam voluntarily accepted the command of God, still less that he had any knowledge that his posterity were to be affected by his conduct; and he was constituted their representative, not by any choice or will on their part, but by the sovereign appointment of God. Thus the transaction is not perfectly analogous to those in which communities or nations have to bear the penalty of actions done by representatives chosen or commissioned by themselves. The notion of a covenant unity and representation of all mankind by the first man does not by itself remove the difficulty arising from their having to suffer the consequences of his sin; and to rely upon it for that purpose is unwise. But it may fairly be used to illustrate the method of the divine government, and to throw some light on what is dark and mysterious in it.

After all, the root of the difficulty lies in the constitution of mankind in families and successive generations. If the human race was to be propagated in that way, it was inevitable that children, and children's children, must be affected, to some degree, by the conduct of their ancestors, and ultimately by that of the first parents of the race. Even were it only by example and imitation, such an influence there must have been, and on the whole this arrangement has been highly favourable to human progress. The only conceivable difference that there could have been is merely one of degree; and we may well believe that the degree in which the destinies of the race have been affected by the conduct of our first parents, according to the Covenant of Works, is that which, all things considered, was the most proper in the view of God's infinite wisdom. This method of federal representation formed the type and preparation for that greater and more perfect covenant, in which an innumerable multitude of sinners are saved and blessed through the righteousness of the one man Jesus Christ, the last Adam, their Covenant Head.

In this broad and comprehensive aspect, the federal unity of the race with its first parents is presented to us in Scripture; and viewed thus, though it cannot solve the mysterious enigma of human history, it gives us large and elevating ideas of the all-embracing plan of God, who "hath shut up all unto disobedience, that He might have mercy on all" (Rom. xi. 32).

The doctrine of the imputation of Adam's sin occupies, in the Protestant theology of the seventeenth century, proportionately much more space and importance than it has in the Bible; and the reason is, that it was believed that whatever view was taken of it must be applied also to the parallel doctrine of the imputation of Christ's righteousness to believers. Hence, also, the importance attached to the difference between what was called mediate and immediate imputation. Some held that we ought to conceive of the corruption which men inherit from Adam as forming the ground or reason of the imputation of his sin; which is accordingly consequent upon, or mediated by, that corruption. This theory was introduced by Placæus of Saumur, and was called Mediate or Consequent Imputation. But the majority of Protestant theologians held that the imputation of guilt was directly grounded on Adam's sin, and antecedent, in the order of nature, to the inheritance of corruption.

This seems a difference on a very obscure point, and of no great moment; but since, in the doctrine of salvation, it is of vital importance to maintain that believers are justified directly on account of Christ, to whom they are united by faith, and not on the ground of their own renewed character, it appeared necessary to hold a similar direct relation between the condemnation of the race and the sin of its first covenant head. It was for this reason that Dr. Chalmers, in his later years, abandoned the theory of mediate imputation, which he had previously adopted from Edwards.[1] On the other hand, those who studied the doctrine of sin by itself, especially if they could not accept the theory either of a realistic or of a federal oneness with Adam, felt that the imputation of his sin needed some ground to justify it; and some statements of Scripture, especially in Ezek. xviii., seemed to make the inheritance of a sinful character such a ground.

[1] See *Institutes of Theology*, Part I. ch. vi.

But these inferences on both sides assume that Scripture analogies are exact and perfect in every point not expressly excepted. If Paul meant to say, that the parallel between Adam and Christ holds in every respect except those in which he says they differ, then the argument for immediate imputation is good; and if the imputation of Adam's sin is exactly analogous to the cases spoken of by Ezekiel, the inference in favour of mediate imputation would be valid. But neither of these assumptions is certain; and as both cannot be true, the probability is that neither is so. It would seem, therefore, that this is a question which, like those of Realism, Creationism, Traducianism, and the like, cannot be decided by Scripture, but must be left open.

One effect of the exaggerated importance and over minute definition given to this doctrine has been, that many theologians, believing that all men inherit depravity from our first parents, have denied entirely the doctrine of the imputation of Adam's sin. Since that doctrine has come to be understood in different senses, which are sometimes very confusing, and has been made the ground of so much extra-scriptural dogmatising, one cannot wonder that they have thought it better to discard it entirely, and to keep to what is much more prominent in the Bible, and much more important for practical and religious purposes. Oosterzee [1] is a very good representative of this form of thought.

[1] See *Christian Dogmatics*, section lxxv.

CHAPTER XII.

ELEMENTS OF HOPE IN MAN'S SINFUL STATE.

WHILE the Christian revelation testifies the state of mankind to be a very sad and deplorable one, and gives a clearer view and a deeper sense of the awfulness of moral evil, as sin against God, and of the strong hold that it has on all men by nature, it does not represent man's condition as at all hopeless. The purpose of its teaching on this subject is, not to drive men to despair, but to lead them to hope and faith in God. Indeed, even some of the dark features in its picture of human sin afford, when rightly viewed, elements of hopefulness.

Thus for one thing, the doctrine that man's sinfulness has come by a fall, and is not a necessary and inevitable evil, inherent in his very nature, as a finite or as a corporeal being, affords ground of hope. If the sinfulness of man had been due to the essential evil of matter, or to the unavoidable limitations of a finite being, or to the necessary contrasts of individual life; then deliverance from it would be absolutely impossible as long as men remain finite, corporeal individuals. But since, according to the Bible, it is due to no such cause; but has proceeded from the free will of a being created upright, and is the corruption of a nature that is in its essence good; deliverance from it is not impossible. The corruption is, indeed, so deep and inveterate, that man cannot deliver himself from it; his salvation must come from God. But his nature is still capable of redemption; the divine image in which he was created, though sadly defaced, may be restored to even more than its original brightness. Even the lowest savage has some idea of God; he has a conscience which, though it may be perverted and blunted, gives a knowledge of moral good and evil, and a heart whose affections may be touched by the revelation of the love of God, as seen in the life and death of Christ.

Again, the doctrine of man's entire inability to deliver himself from the bondage of sin, while it gives a humbling view of his condition, and one that has ever been distasteful to human pride and self-conceit, has yet, as presented in the gospel, a hopeful side. For it is taught in connection with the announcement, that though we have destroyed ourselves, in God is our help found; that He has sent His Son to seek and to save the lost, and sends forth His Holy Spirit to convince us of sin and lead us to Christ, in whom we have forgiveness and renewal. Since we are wholly unable to save ourselves, God in His grace takes this work upon Himself; and if we but trust to Christ as our Saviour, and follow Him as our Lord and Leader, we have an assurance of being delivered from our wretched captivity under sin. If we had power left to save ourselves, it must have depended on our own efforts, and on our success in a hard and unequal conflict, of which the issue could not be certain. But now, since we are helpless, the power that saves us must be God's; and if we have God's power with us, the struggle, though hard, is not uncertain. Victory over sin is within the reach of the most guilty, the most degraded, the veriest slave of vice, if only he will lay hold of God's mercy in Christ, and by His grace turn from sin to God.

This is not merely a doctrine to be received on authority, even that of Christ, it is an actual fact. Salvation is a reality in human experience, as truly as sin. It is a sad and terrible fact that sin reigns; that men and women all around us are under the dominion of evil passions, desires, and habits, worldly, selfish, avaricious, ungodly. But it is no less true and certain, that many men and women all around us have been delivered from this bondage, and have been enabled to deny ungodliness and worldly lusts, and to live soberly, and righteously, and godly.

No candid man can deny that there are, beside all the formalists and hypocrites who disgrace religion, truly sincere, good, pious, loving people, striving against indwelling sin, and, amid many failings, gradually conquering it. These facts are undeniable. But the question is, How have these become more godly and less sinful than others? Is it because they have not been so deeply corrupted; because they have had finer natures, or more genial circumstances; or because human nature not being totally depraved, they have been able, by efforts of will, by heroic self-denial or self-discipline, to make themselves better than others? Oh, if this were so, what hope would there be for those who are of coarser nature, or in less favourable circumstances, or who have not the strength of will or power of endurance to attain such heights of virtue? But since it is not so, but the godly have been saved from sin, as they all thankfully acknowledge, not by their own efforts, but by the grace of God in Jesus Christ; then there is hope for every one; for where sin abounded, grace did much more abound. The existence of any true Christians in the world at all is a practical proof to every sinner that he may be saved from sin, and that he certainly shall be saved if he will but believe on the Lord Jesus Christ, as He is freely offered in the gospel. True, he will not be entirely delivered at once; but he will be entirely forgiven and received into God's favour for Christ's sake as soon as he accepts Him as his Saviour, and he will receive in his soul, through the Holy Spirit, a new affection of love to God and Christ which will have an expulsive power to banish the love of self and the world. Thus the old man, or indwelling sin, will receive its death-blow. But it will not be destroyed magically, without an effort and struggle of his own will. Corruption remains in the regenerate, and is still sinful and hateful to God, as it now is also to themselves. But it shall not have dominion over them; it may struggle long and be hard to overcome, but the earnest Christian will work out his own salvation with fear and trembling, since it is God that worketh in him both to will and to do of His good pleasure.

Further, the Christian doctrine of man's sinful state is hopeful, because of the high ideal which it implies. Any theory that takes a less severe view of human guilt and depravity must lower the standard by which men are to be judged. Absolute sinlessness is not to be required or expected; some sins are venial, and the commission of them is not inconsistent with moral perfection; or sins that are involuntary, that proceed from the natural constitution of a man, he cannot be held responsible for; or desires that are not yielded to by the will, cannot be held sinful; or earnestness and sincerity are all that is needful for Christian perfection : such are some of the ideas adopted by those who shrink from the recognition of man's utter sinfulness. But all these lower the ideal of human character, and in so doing degrade man, and deprive him of the high hope of moral perfection. The teaching that insists on the unbending authority of the law of absolute holiness—" Be ye perfect, as your Father in heaven is perfect;" "Be ye holy, for I am holy;" "Except your righteousness shall exceed the righteousness of the scribes and Pharisees, ye shall in no case enter the kingdom of heaven"—while it stamps man's actual character with more and deeper sinfulness, also honours him, even as he now is, by the very loftiness of the standard it sets before him. The greatness and the blessedness of Christianity are seen, as much in the greatness of its commands as of its promises. For in Christ the commands are promises, since God gives what He commands. That high ideal of holiness need not be despaired of by any. It is, indeed, beyond the power of any, even the best, to attain by his own will or efforts; but, by the grace of God in Christ Jesus, it may be attained even by the worst; and whosoever will trust to Christ as his Saviour shall assuredly attain it.

Further, the circumstance that all men have been involved in sin and suffering through the fall of our first parents, and that God deals with the human race as one whole, has also a hopeful as well as a dark side. It makes the ruin that has come through the first sin of man most terrible and widespread, but it also shows us how a salvation as far-reaching is possible. For, as Paul teaches, it is in the same way as we suffer for the disobedience of the first Adam that we are saved by the obedience of the last Adam. If there had been no room in the divine government for the principle of solidarity, and the representation of many by one ; if God dealt with His creatures purely and only as individuals, so that no one should suffer in consequence of the wrong-doing of any other : then it would be equally impossible that any one could benefit by another's good deeds. Had that been so, not only would a great source of sympathy, and kindliness, and love among men have been closed up, but that gracious covenant would have been excluded, by which God, for the sake of the obedience and sacrifice of Christ, freely forgives and receives into His favour those who believe in Him, and also extends a gracious forbearance and a free offer of mercy to all men.

But now we are involved in a common ruin, the more sad and awful because it is as universal as humanity; but by its very universality we learn to feel with and for our fellow-men, to take heed not only to what we receive from our ancestors, but to what we transmit to those who come after us, and to believe that as sin has reigned unto death, so grace shall reign through righteousness unto eternal life by Jesus Christ our Lord.

Here, too, they are actual facts with which we have to do. The miseries of human life are realities, and the Christian doctrine that traces them back to sin as their cause, and that to an inherited inclination to evil, is borne out by facts. In sober truth, the world is manifestly under the displeasure of God; and that justly, for it is an evil world. But it is equally plain that it has not been cast off by God, nay, that it receives very remarkable tokens of His mercy and grace. It is a world lying in the wicked one, a world of which Satan is prince ; yet it is declared at the same time that God loves it, and has given His only-begotten Son to be the Saviour of the world. The true humanity does not consist of those who yield to Satan and obey him as their prince, but of those who are in Christ; they are the true seed of the woman. Christ, and not Adam, is the true Head of humanity, and all that was lost by Adam's sin is restored, and far more than restored, by the life and death of Christ.

www.ingramcontent.com/pod-product-compliance
Lightning Source LLC
Chambersburg PA
CBHW022136160426
43197CB00009B/1307